Some Things I've Learned Since I Knew It All

Cycle B Sermons for
Pentecost Sunday Through Proper 13
Based on the Gospel Texts

Ron Lavin

CSS Publishing Company, Inc.
Lima, Ohio

SOME THINGS I'VE LEARNED SINCE I KNEW IT ALL

FIRST EDITION
Copyright © 2014
by CSS Publishing Co., Inc.

Library of Congress Cataloging-in-Publication Data

Lavin, Ronald J.
  Some things I've learned since I knew it all (gospel sermons, B cycle, Pentecost) / by Ron Lavin. -- FIRST EDITION.
    pages cm
  Includes bibliographical references.
  ISBN 0-7880-2777-8 (alk. paper)
  1. Bible. Mark--Sermons. 2. Bible. John--Sermons. 3. Pentecost--Sermons. 4. Common lectionary (1992). Year B. I. Title.

  BS2585.54.L38 2014
  252'64--dc23

                                                    2013041515

For more information about CSS Publishing Company resources, visit our website at www. csspub.com, email us at csr@csspub.com, or call (800) 241-4056.

e-book:
ISBN-13: 978-0-7880-2778-9
ISBN-10: 0-7880-2778-6

ISBN-13: 978-0-7880-2777-2
ISBN-10: 0-7880-2777-8

PRINTED IN USA

*This book is dedicated to
Rod and Caroline Anderson,
Mel and Jane Keischnick,
Martha Love,
Jonathan Jacob,
Bud Potter,
and many other friends
from whom I have learned
valuable lessons about life.*

Other Books by Ron Lavin

Mission, Evangelism, and Small Groups

Witness (The Reign of God and Missional Churches Today)
Way to Grow! (Dynamic Church Growth Through Small Groups)
You Can Grow in a Small Group
Koinonia Groups (A Strategy for Renewal)

The Gospels

The Eagle (Gospel of John)
The Servant Lord (Gospel of Mark, electronic book only)

The Another Look Series

Only The Lonely (Another Look at Loneliness)
People Who Met Jesus (Another Look at the Suffering, Death, and Resurrection of the Lord)
The Big Ten (Another Look at the Ten Commandments)
Saving Grace (Another Look at the Word and Sacraments)
Abba (Another Look at the Lord's Prayer)
Stories To Remember (Another Look at the Parables of Jesus)
I Believe; Help My Unbelief (Another Look at the Apostles' Creed)

Published Sermons

"Some Things I've Learned Since I Knew It All," Pentecost season, Cycle B, 11 sermons
Sermons on the Gospels, Pentecost 2, Cycle C, 11 sermons
Sermons on the First Lessons, Cycle B, 6 sermons
Augsburg Sermons, Gospel Series, B, 8 sermons
Augsburg Sermons, Gospel Series, C, "The Holy Spirit And Hospitality"
Augsburg Sermons 2, Gospel Series, B, "A Foretaste Of The Feast To Come"

Augsburg Sermons 2, Gospel Series, C, "Is There Life After Thirty?"

Augsburg Sermons, Old Testament Lessons, B, "The Lord Is My Shepherd"

"In Sure And Certain Hope," funeral sermon, Kim's Wish Come True

Other Books

Turning Griping Into Gratitude (The Psalms)

Empty Spaces; Empty Places (Written with Constance Sorenson)

The Advocate

The Great I AM

Previews of Coming Attractions

Alone/Together

You Can't Start A Car With A Cross

Roots And Wings

The Human Chain For Divine Grace (editor)

Jesus In Stained Glass

Jesus Christ, The Liberator (Written with Bill Grimmer, MD)

Hey Mom, Look At Me!

Preface

This series of sermons is for Pentecost Sunday and the season of Pentecost through Proper 13.

The theme running through this series is the work of the Holy Spirit, our Advocate. The Advocate can take a written text and through the preaching of the gospel turn it in our minds and hearts in such a way that the text comes alive. That is one of the most important things I've learned in life.

In other words, the Advocate has revealed that preaching the gospel text can be a channel from heaven to earth, from God to God's people. As you consider these sermons, consider too how the Holy Spirit can make them live in the practical lives of the people who hear them. It isn't enough to state the truth of God's word. We preachers must always ask, "How can we contribute to the possibility of this word from God actually making a difference in someone's life?"

Phillips Brooks once observed, "Some preachers give lectures on medicine to people who are desperate for medicine." People want and need more than good ideas. People want and need medicine of God's living word; not words about something that was only true 2,000 years ago.

How do we preachers make the word come alive for people? We can't! That's the work of the Holy Spirit. However, there is something we can do, something we must do. We can and must consider more than the truth of the text: We must consider the way the text intersects our life and the lives of the hearers.

The Advocate has revealed through the life of Jesus that stories can help. Parables can help. Real-life situations, described with colorful detail can help. We preachers must pray that we stand aside and let God convert, change, and reach the hearts and minds of God's people. We must pray that we will be transparent, not getting in the way of the Holy Spirit,

God's Advocate to us and for us.

Since the time I was a young man and thought I knew it all, these are a few of the things I have learned. In addition, I've learned that it is the Advocate who calls us to faith. We don't call ourselves and we don't achieve faith. We receive faith. As a young man, there was too much Ron and not enough God in my faith formula. Anybody else like that?

Since I thought I knew it all, I have discovered that the Advocate gathers us into the faith community. When I was young, there was too much individualism in my life philosophy and not enough community. I have learned that faith is never a matter of individual effort. Faith is personal, but never private. Faith must always be developed and nurtured in the faith community because we are so easily deceived. Pride comes before the fall every time. The correctives are in the community.

Since I thought I knew everything, I discovered that the Advocate enlightens us with his gifts. In other words, if anything I write, preach, or teach is good, it is God at work, in spite of me. If what is written, preached, or taught is not so good, that's Ron. If it works to the glory of God, it is all gift, all grace, all God's Spirit that is doing the work. That Holy Spirit of God gives spiritual gifts to people to get God's work done. When I started out as a Christian, I was only vaguely familiar with that reality.

Since I thought I knew everything, I discovered that the Advocate sanctifies us by keeping us together in dynamic fellowship with Jesus Christ and one another. That's called *koinonia* in the New Testament. When I was young, before I became a Christian, I didn't understand that at all. I saw the church as a group of like-minded people with which I needed no contact at all.

It's been a while since I thought I knew it all, but remnants of that sin still pop up from time to time. When they do, I try to remind myself that God's Advocate calls, gathers, enlightens, and sanctifies us in true faith as Martin Luther explains in *The Small Catechism*. Those verbs outline some of the things I have learned since I was foolish enough to think I knew it all.

One more thing I have learned. There is no room in life for pride, arrogance, or boasting. We never even come close to knowing it all and whatever we know can be either good or bad, since we have both good and bad within us. As a wise old man once said, "It's like there are two dogs always fighting inside us. The one is called good; the other evil." An inquisitive young man asked the wise man, "Which dog wins the fight?" The wise man replied, "That depends on which dog you feed."

A person can act in good ways, sometimes even very good ways. But every person is also bad, sometimes very bad. Even when we do something good, there is a tendency to feed the bad dog of pride, arrogance, and boasting. The two-footed handiwork of God was made in God's image. We have something of God within us. That's why we long for God, like a deer pants for water. God's two-footed handiwork has two natures — good as he was intended to be and evil as he is, having a fallen nature. Watch for both the law and the gospel in these eleven sermons. They both deal with human nature and God's ways.

The attempt here and in all preaching is to glorify God, not human beings. The attempt here is to deal with our two natures that are in conflict with one another and to be more charitable in our judgments. "There's so much good in the worst of us and so much bad in the best of us, that it doesn't behoove any of us to be judgmental about the rest of us" (Anonymous).

John Adams, one of the prime movers of the Declaration of Independence and the second President of the United

States, drove home the biblical truth of the double nature of human beings with these words to his grandson John: "No pride, John, no pride." John Adams also wrote to another family member: "You are singular in your suspicion that you know but little. The longer I live, the more I read, the more patiently I think, and the more anxiously I inquire, the less I seem to know.... Do justly. Love mercy. Walk humbly. This is enough...."[1]

Above all things I've learned since I thought I knew it all is that the more I know, the more I know that I don't know very much.

Ron Lavin
written July 4, 2013
the 237th anniversary of the Declaration of Independence

---

1. David McCullough, *John Adams* (New York: Simon and Schuster, 2001), p. 659.

Table of Contents

Pentecost Sunday
John 15:26-27; 16:4-15

"When the Advocate comes, whom I will send to you from the Father, the Spirit of truth who comes from the Father, he will testify on my behalf. You also are to testify because you have been with me from the beginning...." But I have said these things to you so that when their hour comes you may remember that I told you about them. "I did not say these things to you from the beginning, because I was with you. But now I am going to him who sent me; yet none of you asks me, 'Where are you going?' But because I have said these things to you, sorrow has filled your hearts. Nevertheless I tell you the truth: it is to your advantage that I go away, for if I do not go away, the Advocate will not come to you; but if I go, I will send him to you. And when he comes, he will prove the world wrong about sin and righteousness and judgment: about sin, because they do not believe in me; about righteousness, because I am going to the Father and you will see me no longer; about judgment, because the ruler of this world has been condemned. I still have many things to say to you, but you cannot bear them now. When the Spirit of truth comes, he will guide you into all the truth; for he will not speak on his own, but will speak whatever he hears, and he will declare to you the things that are to come. He will glorify me, because he will take what is mine and declare it to you. All that the Father has is mine. For this reason I said that he will take what is mine and declare it to you."

The Advocate and the Street Where You Live

According to the dictionary, an advocate is "a powerful and influential person who defends or maintains a cause or proposal on our behalf." Someone working for us and on our behalf can be very beneficial when we are in some kind of difficulty or trouble. Someone working for us and on our behalf in life with integrity has value beyond description. In other words, a strong human advocate can save us from dire situations in which we might find ourselves.

Let's take the case of a man, let's call him John, who was accused of murder. He was arrested and went to trial. Having a strong lawyer who has integrity and who can defend John was a matter of life and death. Instead, John had a lawyer who met with him only once and who never asked John how he wanted to plea. In addition, the week before the trial, John's lawyer was arrested on a morals charge for having sex with an underaged girl. That lack of a trustworthy advocate led to John's conviction of murder. Just twelve hours before he was scheduled to lose his life in the electric chair, John got a "stay of execution" from the governor of Indiana. The plea of "incompetent counsel" was finally heard by the right people. The importance of having a lawyer who can properly represent us and advocate for us is essential for our justice system. In John's case it was a matter of life and death.

Whether or not you will ever need a competent lawyer to represent you in a trial, you do need a competent and strong Advocate for life. That is what is being described in our text.

15

Jesus says, "When the Advocate comes, whom I will send to you from the Father — the Spirit of truth who goes out from the Father — he will testify about me" (John 15:26).

This testimony of the Advocate, much more than the testimony and defense by a dedicated, strong, and tough lawyer, is a matter of life and death. The Holy Spirit, our Advocate, makes the difference between eternal life and eternal death by leading us to faith in Jesus.

The Holy Spirit testified to the apostles about Jesus Christ. At the time of Pentecost, there were eleven apostles. Judas, the twelfth apostle, had committed suicide after his betrayal of Jesus. Paul who was eventually viewed as the twelfth apostle was not a part of the picture yet. On Pentecost Day, a harvest festival for the Jews, the Holy Spirit descended upon the apostles and other believers and the church of Jesus Christ was born. The Advocate confirmed the meaning of what had happened to Jesus and the apostles became the pillars on which the emerging community of God, called the church, was built.

The Holy Spirit testified to the early Christians about Jesus Christ. Using Peter's amazing, confident speech on Pentecost about the risen Lord Jesus Christ, the Advocate brought 3,000 people to faith. How? By convincing them of "sin, righteousness, and judgment" (John 16:8-11).

Convinced of sin? Yes, they were. Peter helped them understand their sin and need for a Savior. He knew his own need for forgiveness of sin. He had denied even knowing Jesus outside the high priest's home. He knew that where there is no repentance for sin, there is no new life. Peter could preach about sin and forgiveness because he knew the experience firsthand. So did the other apostles who had deserted Jesus in his hour of need. Peter understood the need for people being convicted of their sinfulness and the need for repentance. Thousands were turned around that day. They were turned back to God.

Convinced of righteousness? Yes, they were. Peter's sermon converted the people who heard the gospel. The people saw that Peter was right. More importantly, they saw that Jesus was right. He was the promised righteous one, the Messiah, the fulfillment of the longing of the people of Israel.

Convinced of judgment? Yes, they were. Peter described the generation in vivid terms with the clear implication that those who did not turn away from the sinful tendencies of their society would have to face the judgment of almighty God. He said, "Save yourselves from this corrupt generation" (Acts 2:40 NIV). In other translations, the word "corrupt" is translated "crooked" (RSV), "perverted" (Phillips translation), and "wicked" (TEV). That's judgment on sin in the present age with the promise of ultimate judgment in the hereafter. The Holy Spirit testified to the apostles.

The Holy Spirit also testifies to us today. How? Through the preaching of the word. Every sermon needs both law and gospel in it. We all need to hear both judgment and grace. In times gone by there was so much law in the preaching and teaching of churches that there was a great imbalance. Today, the imbalance is in the opposite direction. Preachers tend to go lightly or not at all into that dangerous zone of punishment for sin. For many, the Ten Commandments have become the Ten Suggestions with an understanding that these ten were related to how things were years ago and have little or nothing to do with us today. For example, contrary to popular belief, God's last name is not "Damn." Concretely, no matter how many people disagree, sex outside of marriage is sinful. Unfortunately, idolatry appears repeatedly, whether or not we have golden calves. That's bad news.

Of course, the gospel of grace for sinners is good news. Of course, God is more willing to forgive than we are to ask for forgiveness. Of course, the undeserving prodigal son was welcomed home by his loving father and God is better than any human father could ever be. Yes, yes, yes. But without getting in touch with our true guilt followed by repentance (the prodigal's turn around to face God) there is no forgiveness. Grace is free, but it isn't cheap. It cost Jesus his life.

The sin, righteousness, and judgment theme of the Bible encourages and enforces the possibility of new life in Christ for people today. Luther put it directly in *The Small Catechism*. He tells us in the Explanation of the Second Article of the Apostles' Creed that we are called to salvation in the name of Jesus Christ, true God, true man, and our Lord. Then he says, "I believe that I cannot by my own reason or strength come to the Lord Jesus Christ or believe in him, but through Holy Spirit...." In other words, I am commanded to believe in Jesus for salvation, but I cannot do what I am commanded to do. The Holy Spirit, my Advocate, is the one who brings me to faith in Christ and keeps me there. No credit goes to me; all credit for salvation goes to the Advocate of God.

What is my contribution to my salvation? It is my sin, the very sin from which I must be saved. What's God's contribution? It is the suffering and death of Jesus Christ on the cross to which the Holy Spirit points me and leads me. That I have an Advocate in the Holy Spirit means that God fulfills what God demands. Luther calls that the "joyous exchange."

Because God made me in his image, he gave me the power to resist him and his ways. To be made in God's image means that I have the freedom to resist or accept what God has done for me, to ignore my Creator, or love him in response to his love for me. My sin is to use my God-given freedom to turn away from the God who loves me. It is like God has written a check for a million dollars, but I have the freedom to sign the back of the check or never sign or cash it. Who would be so foolish as not to endorse the gift? Yet many do just that.

All people have received an enormous and gracious gift from God. That gift is like receiving a check for a million dollars. Some people put that check in a drawer and never cash it. Some deny that they have ever received that gift. The gift of God, worth much more than a million dollars, is the gift of eternal life given freely to those who believe in and receive the benefits of the death of God's Son on the cross. To neglect that gift of God is to sin greatly by taking God for granted. To take God for granted and not endorse and appreciate the gift of his Son is the sin against the Holy Spirit, what the Bible calls the unforgivable sin. The Advocate leads us to saving faith in Christ. To renounce the Holy Spirit is to pronounce judgment against ourselves.

The Holy Spirit leads us to saving faith. That Spirit, our Advocate, also inspires us as witnesses and guides us through the wilderness of life.

The text, John 15 and 16, originally applied to the people of the first century. The text also deals with us today. In the first century, the Advocate called, gathered, enlightened, and sanctified the disciples of Jesus Christ. That's also true for twenty-first-century disciples.

After telling us how the Holy Spirit testifies to us about faith, Jesus says, "And you also must testify, for you have been with me from the beginning" (John 15:27). In John 16:13 Jesus says, "But when he, the Spirit of truth, comes, he will guide you into all the truth."

In other words, the Advocate justifies us before God and sanctifies us as well. As sanctified sinners we are called to share faith with others. That's called witnessing. Every Christian is not an evangelist (only *some* as Ephesians 4:11 says), but *every Christian is a witness* (Acts 1:8). Evangelists are called to *declare the gospel*; witnesses are called to *share the gospel*. That may seem like a small distinction, but it is an important one.

Our job as Christian witnesses isn't to convert people. Only the Holy Spirit can bring a person to saving faith in Christ. Our job is to provide the context for people to come to faith by being invitational, inviting people to come to worship, a Bible study, or a social program at church where they can meet Christians. Our job is to introduce or re-introduce them to Jesus by words and deeds. Yes, but isn't this all just theological jargon and theory? People want something real, something to take home to the street where they live.

What about the practical side of things? What about real life? What about the street where you live? When Jesus dealt head on with practical problems in real-life settings, he often told stories that brought home God's truths to his hearers. As we try to ask the tough questions about witnessing and God's Advocate, the Holy Spirit, maybe a story will help.

Her name was Hanna. She had a college roommate named Sue. Sue didn't go to church anymore. "I'm a good person without church," Sue said, "There are a lot of hypocrites in the church and I don't like being around hypocrites. I believe there is a god, but won't any old god do? There are lots of different religions. I'll get around to one of them someday." Sue was a humanist, a good person without God. No amount of urging on Hanna's part made any apparent difference. After two years of rooming together, Sue read a letter from home telling her that her mother was dying with breast cancer.

The two young women sat and cried together until there were no more tears left. Then they talked. "You are always telling me that God is so good. Where is God now?" Sue shouted. "Why? Why? Why?"

"There are no simple answers to the question of suffering and death," Hanna replied. "But it is for times like these when you are experiencing suffering that Jesus died on the cross. He took our suffering upon himself. He suffered for us so that we need never suffer alone. He goes through what we go through before it happens to us. He is the suffering servant. We don't know the answer to the question 'Why?' but we do know the answer to the question 'How?' How can we get through this suffering and death itself? We do it through the suffering servant. I don't know all the answers, but I know someone who does. His name is Jesus."

Sue did not turn to Jesus Christ for comfort that night but she did think about what her roommate said, especially in her mother's last days. After the funeral for her mother, she told Hanna that she wasn't ready to become a Christian but she was thinking about things from a different perspective now, especially because of what her mother told her before she died.

"What was that?" Hanna asked.

"Mom told me she was on a journey and that Jesus was leading her through the wilderness of pain and suffering. She believed she was on her way to the Promised Land. Then I remembered your words, Hanna, when you told me that we didn't know why we suffer, but we do know how to deal with suffering and death. Mom knew how to deal with her tribulations. I don't, but maybe someday I will. I know I'm missing something but I'm not sure just what it is. Thanks for your words. They didn't bring Mom back but they helped me get through her death. You are a real friend and advocate. Your words meant more to me than you can imagine."

Hanna said, "I don't know where the words came from. I guess they must have come from the Holy Spirit because I am not smart enough to say all that."

At this writing, Sue is still an outsider to the Christian faith, but some doors have been opened. Through Hanna, Sue has met some new friends who, like Hanna, are advocates for God. Will Sue personally appropriate what Jesus has accomplished for her on the cross? Will she become a

Christian? Will she accept what the Advocate of God is leading her to believe and do? Will she become an advocate for God? God only knows, but what we know is that the Advocate is at work in Sue's life. That is the promise of the one who never breaks a promise.

Trinity Sunday
John 3:1-17

Now there was a Pharisee named Nicodemus, a leader of the Jews. He came to Jesus by night and said to him, "Rabbi, we know that you are a teacher who has come from God; for no one can do these signs that you do apart from the presence of God." Jesus answered him, "Very truly, I tell you, no one can see the kingdom of God without being born from above." Nicodemus said to him, "How can anyone be born after having grown old? Can one enter a second time into the mother's womb and be born?" Jesus answered, "Very truly, I tell you, no one can enter the kingdom of God without being born of water and Spirit. What is born of the flesh is flesh, and what is born of the Spirit is spirit. Do not be astonished that I said to you, 'You must be born from above.' The wind blows where it chooses, and you hear the sound of it, but you do not know where it comes from or where it goes. So it is with everyone who is born of the Spirit." Nicodemus said to him, "How can these things be?" Jesus answered him, "Are you a teacher of Israel, and yet you do not understand these things?" "Very truly, I tell you, we speak of what we know and testify to what we have seen; yet you do not receive our testimony. If I have told you about earthly things and you do not believe, how can you believe if I tell you about heavenly things? No one has ascended into heaven except the one who descended from heaven, the Son of Man. And just as Moses lifted up the serpent in the wilderness, so must the Son of Man be lifted up, that whoever believes in him may have eternal life. For God so loved the world that he gave his only Son, so that everyone who believes in him may not perish but may have eternal life. Indeed, God did not send the Son into the world to condemn the world, but in order that the world might be saved through him."

What Does the Kingdom of God Have to Do With Anything Today?

It started with a question in the form of a statement. It ended with the most memorable words in the Bible. In between, there were many mysteries, not the least of which was the declarative statement by Jesus about rebirth and the kingdom of God. I'm talking about the story of the nocturnal meeting of Nicodemus, the member of the Jewish supreme court, with Jesus, who according to John's gospel was the dynamic and unpredictable messianic ruler of the universe, the word of God become flesh and blood who came to teach us about the kingdom of God.

The implied question of Nicodemus hid behind his statement: "Rabbi, we know that you are a teacher who has come from God. For no one could perform the signs you are doing if God were not with him" (John 3:2). The implied question was "a powerful teacher, yes, but how much more are you?" Nicodemus asked the question of the ages: "Just who do you claim to be?"

Notice two reversals in our story. First, Jesus neither comments on Nicodemus' statement nor does he answer the implied question. Instead, he completely changes the subject. Based on his knowledge of what Nicodemus really needs to know, Jesus tells him: "Very truly, I tell you, no one can see the kingdom of God unless they are born again" (John 3:3).

This first reversal must have shocked the learned judge from the Sanhedrin. "What is he talking about?" he thought.

Defensively he said: "How can someone be born when they are old?" (John 3:4). In other words, "Jesus, would you like to have a theological discussion about the kingdom of God and this idea of rebirth you are raising?" Effectively, Jesus said, "No" to the proposed discussion of theology. Jesus said, "Very truly I tell you, no one can enter the kingdom of God unless they are born of water and the Spirit" (John 3:5). In other words, Jesus is saying, "No, I am not interested in an intellectual discussion at all. I want to talk about you."

This second reversal takes Nicodemus, and us, completely off guard. After saying, "I don't want to talk about ideas at all." Jesus says, "You may be inquisitive about who I am, but I want you to think about who you are and what you need from God. You are a sinner. You need forgiveness, salvation, and spiritual rebirth." That's what I call a staggering confrontation with the truth for the well-intentioned religious leader and for us.

Talk about shocking reversals! These opening volleys in the Nicodemus story would knock your socks off if you were standing there in the shadows listening to the exchange. So would the concluding words of the story. These words at the end of the story are so familiar to us that we can almost forget how shocking they must have seemed when Nicodemus first heard them. Again, put yourself into the story, as if you are standing, hidden in the shadows, overhearing these familiar and beloved words for the first time: "For God so loved the world that he gave his one and only Son, that whoever believes in him shall not perish but have eternal life" (John 3:16).

The love of God? God's Son? Born again of water and the Spirit? All these terms and ideas are about the kingdom of God? If you can hear the words as if you are hearing them for the first time, you must be asking, like Nicodemus must have asked, "What's it all about?" This appears to be an enigma wrapped in a mystery in a dark corner of an ancient and ambiguous story unrelated to real life today. What in the world does this kingdom story have to do with our lives or with anything?

Intrigue lurks between each of Jesus' statements to the inquisitive judge. Maybe the place to start is to peel away the outer shell of this mystery by looking at what the words meant for Nicodemus. Then we can examine what they might mean for us today.

When a confused Nicodemus asks Jesus: "How can this be?" (John 3:9), Jesus begins to explain the meaning by calling Nicodemus, "Israel's teacher" (John 3:10). The implied meaning is that as a religious teacher of the Jews, you should understand these things.

First, the kingdom of God is God's rule over us for our own good. "Nicodemus, you know all about the kingdom from your study of scriptures. The Bible is filled with references to God's rule over us. The scriptures tell us of the coming *day of the Lord* when righteousness shall rule and justice shall finally be done, when evil will no longer hold sway and good will emerge completely from the shadows. You know, Nicodemus, it is there in the law. It's there in the prophets."

God doesn't rule over us like some eastern potentate who conquers us to make us his slaves. No, God wants to rule over us with love for our own good. We aren't who we were intended to be until we come under the one who created us. When the great rebellion took place and Adam and Eve disobeyed God, the pattern was set for all of us. Misusing our freedom, abusing our potential for good by turning it into something demonic, we left the rule of God only to discover that if God doesn't rule over us, something or someone else will. You know, Nicodemus, you are a teacher of these things.

God wants only the best for us. He knows that we get the

best only when we live as we were created to be, that is, as his children. When we, like prodigals, take him for granted and wander off, we are miserable and we have to face the consequences of this disobedience. You know, Nicodemus, you are a teacher of these things.

God loves us. He doesn't want us to come to harm. No good father or mother wants evil for their children. How much more God loves us than any human can love his or her child! How much more, Nicodemus? You know. You are a teacher of these things.

Listen from the shadows as Jesus is saying something like this to Nicodemus: "You are a teacher of Israel, and as such you know a lot, but there is more to know. As a teacher of Israel, you must learn something more. 'God so loved the world that he gave his one and only Son that whoever believes in him shall have eternal life.' That's who I am. That's what I am doing here on earth. I am the Son of God, doing the work of God that people, including you, Nicodemus, might have eternal life."

"Think, Nicodemus, there is more to know. As you know and teach the story of Moses lifting up the snake in the wilderness so that the people who have sinned may look up and live, so the day is coming when I will be lifted up on the cross and those who look up will have eternal life. Think, Nicodemus; that time is coming and remember these words when that time comes."

That's what the kingdom of God is all about. God wants to rule over us from his place of ultimate authority because he knows what is best for us. He made us in his own image. We only fulfill the potential of that image of God within us as we come to submission to his will and ways. Yes, Nicodemus, that's what the kingdom of God is all about.

According to tradition, Nicodemus did in fact have a chance to remember these words. After the crucifixion and resurrection, he remembered what Jesus said, and he believed what Jesus told him. He became a Christian and a leader in the infant Christian church. That's the good news about Nicodemus who first heard what has been called "the gospel within the gospel." That "gospel within the gospel" summarizes the whole of the Christian faith. Children memorize it. Artists set it to music or paint it in pictures. People hold on to it for dear life. "God so loved the world that he gave his one and only Son that whoever believes in him shall have eternal life." That's what the kingdom of God is all about — coming under the banner of God's love by surrendering to Christ as Lord and Savior by the power of the Holy Spirit, experiencing forgiveness and new life, though we in no way deserve what we receive. You have been in the shadows, listening to these words and hearing the responses of Nicodemus. Now it is time for you to come out of the shadows, step into the light, and hear the words of Jesus spoken to you.

Is it possible that you can step out of the shadows from which you have been watching Nicodemus and Jesus, from which you have been listening to their words? Is it possible that you can step out of the shadows into the story? Can you now hear the words as if addressed to you? Yes, I believe since God created you, Jesus died for you, and the Holy Spirit is alive and well, working in you to come to a deeper faith and giving guidance for your life. Yes, I believe that you can step into this Bible story personally. In other words, I believe the kingdom of God, God's reign over us for our own good is possible to experience today. Can you appropriate what has been accomplished for you in Christ? Yes, I believe the word of God can come alive for you today.

It's Trinity Sunday. We have the possibility of returning to the God who created us by appropriating what Jesus accomplished on the cross for us by the power of the Holy Spirit who brings us to faith and faithfulness beyond our wildest dreams.

Like Nicodemus, we experience something different than we deserve or expect. Like him, we are called to faith and faithfulness beyond our ability or strength to fully understand. In addition, we have the possibility of experiencing the love of God which is beyond words to fully describe.

First, as we come before Jesus and enter the story, we notice that he doesn't answer all the questions we raise. He does more. He tells us what we need to know not what we think we need to know. We come to the presence of Jesus with one set of expectations and often find that our preconceptions are burst like so many precarious bubbles fluttering in the air. In other words, we come into the light of Christ with the distinct possibility that we will come to know a great reversal.

Another Bible story may help us connect with the reversal in this story. A Samaritan woman, despised by the Jews, living in sin with a man who was not her husband, expected to draw some water from a well. Instead, she met a man named Jesus who told her about the water that wells up to eternal life and that she could personally be a part of this new life.

Staggered by Jesus' words which showed that he knew all about her life and her sins, she tried to get the spotlight off herself by posing a theological question. Should we worship on the mountain in Samaria or in Jerusalem? Jesus would have none of it. He saw through the thin veil she erected just like he saw through the curtain Nicodemus tried to hide behind. Stopping ever so briefly at the question of where to worship, Jesus brought her face-to-face with the question of faith as she raised the question of the coming Messiah. "I who speak to you am he," he said (John 4:26).

By the time she ran into town to tell everyone she had met the Messiah and that they should come and meet him too, she described her great reversal like this, "He (Jesus) told me everything I've ever done" implying, "he still accepted me." In other words, "I found someone (or rather, he found me) and he loved me unconditionally even though I am a sinner who doesn't deserve his love." Jesus answered the real question of acceptance. That's the first thing we notice.

Second, when we step out of the shadows into the story, we can discover the same love that Nicodemus heard described in unforgettable words and the Samaritan woman experienced in the story of her serendipitous experience of Jesus. We can step right into the love of God which comes to us when we do not expect it or deserve it. A story from today may help to drive home the point of God's personal, powerful, and profound love for sinners.

Her name was Gert Behanna. Her father, who was very wealthy, had high expectations for her. He thought she would be smart enough to discover the cure for cancer. Her mother was beautiful. Gert was not. After becoming an alcoholic and drug addict and failing at three marriages, Gert tried to commit suicide. When she failed at that, she was told by her doctor that she should see a psychiatrist. She replied, "I don't need a psychiatrist. I need God."

In her biography, *God Isn't Dead* (both a book and a Hollywood movie), Gert says, "I don't know where that statement came from. I didn't know anything about the Bible. I didn't even know anyone who said they were a Christian, but somewhere someone must have dropped a seed. I didn't do anything about it when I said it, but later I met my first Christians. I got drunk to meet them which is more of a comment on us as Christians than us as drunks. They were kind enough to listen to my story about how I had been mistreated by my husbands and my father, but then they said something that shocked me. They said, "Gert, why don't you turn your troubles over to God?" And they meant it. Things that are meant are heard.

When Gert turned her troubles over to God, she found a new life. She gave away her enormous wealth and went around the world telling her story to auditoriums filled with the down and out ("bums like me") as well as the up and out, churches filled with overflowing crowds and individual men and women who were led to a touch of eternal life in Jesus Christ by this woman who was born again like Nicodemus.

Step into that story too. Feel the pulse of what it means to become a new person by faith in Christ. God, the Father, created Gert; God, the Son, redeemed her; and God, the Holy Spirit, empowered her to turn to God when her life had fallen apart. You can turn around too. If your life is falling apart, you can step into this story. If your life is going along well, you can still step into this story. It is a story for everyone. We all need the love of God. That is the second theme of John 3:1-17.

Third, you can step out of the shadows and into the story of Nicodemus and personally believe the words you know by heart. "God so loved the world that he sent his one and only Son...." The words are so familiar that we are apt to take them for granted. Familiarity with words often obscures their meaning, sometimes even breeding contempt.

His name was Ralph. He was a regular at church services, often serving as an usher. He had even served one term on the church council. When asked by a Chinese student from a nearby university if he was a Christian, he said, "Of course I'm a Christian. My father was even a pastor." The young girl said softly, "In China, there are no 'of course' Christians."

That got Ralph thinking about his faith. He had grown up in the church and had been baptized and confirmed. He had been born again in the waters of baptism, but he felt like he had lost something somewhere along the way. Ralph knew something was missing. "Maybe I'm an 'of course' Christian," he said to a Christian friend. A sermon his pastor had preached had started what he later called an awakening. The Chinese student had helped him see there was more to Christianity than just going to church. No big conversion event happened in Ralph's life, but on a retreat he felt a big burden move from his shoulders. Peace with God replaced it. "I really want Christ to rule my life," he told his pastor. "That's what the kingdom of God is all about," his pastor said. "Remember, the title of our retreat is From Membership to Discipleship."

It started with a question, "Am I just an 'of course' believer?" It ended with an overwhelming sense that God loves us when we don't deserve it. In between, Ralph experienced many temptations and mysteries.

The story of Nicodemus encourages ordinary people like Ralph to move from just being church members to being disciples of the Lord Jesus Christ. Ordinary people thus become extraordinary kingdom of God people. What does the kingdom of God have to do with life and hope?

Proper 5
Pentecost 2
Ordinary Time 10
Mark 3:20-35

... and the crowd came together again, so that they could not even eat. When his family heard it, they went out to restrain him, for people were saying, "He has gone out of his mind." And the scribes who came down from Jerusalem said, "He has Beelzebul, and by the ruler of the demons he casts out demons." And he called them to him, and spoke to them in parables, "How can Satan cast out Satan? If a kingdom is divided against itself, that kingdom cannot stand. And if a house is divided against itself, that house will not be able to stand. And if Satan has risen up against himself and is divided, he cannot stand, but his end has come. But no one can enter a strong man's house and plunder his property without first tying up the strong man; then indeed the house can be plundered. Truly I tell you, people will be forgiven for their sins and whatever blasphemies they utter; but whoever blasphemes against the Holy Spirit can never have forgiveness, but is guilty of an eternal sin" — for they had said, "He has an unclean spirit." Then his mother and his brothers came; and standing outside, they sent to him and called him. A crowd was sitting around him; and they said to him, "Your mother and your brothers and sisters are outside, asking for you." And he replied, "Who are my mother and my brothers?" And looking at those who sat around him, he said, "Here are my mother and my brothers! Whoever does the will of God is my brother and sister and mother."

Family Ties and Good-byes

Jesus experienced family ties and good-byes. So do we.

According to Mark 3:20-35, Jesus was about to be confronted by his frustrated and conflicted family as crowds gathered around him to hear his stories, behold his miracles, and observe with great interest the conflicts he had with religious leaders from Jerusalem. Conflict. But there were also good, tender, and beautiful joys in Jesus' family. Look at the tenderness at the time of his birth.

Good-byes and ties. All families have stress, as well as happiness, times of anger as well as times of joy, times of agony and times of ecstasy, times of good-bye as well as times when ties bind us together in bonds that seem unbreakable. We can all identify with both the ties and good-byes in Jesus' story, though the reasons for our joys and stresses may be quite different than those in his life.

Our family joys often include good times when we are children — vacations, play times with parents, special birthdays, and holidays. When marriage comes, it is often accompanied by smiles, tears of joy, blessings, affirmations, and congratulations. Family joys often include a baby being born. Babies usually bring big, broad smiles, a sense of mystery and wonder beyond words at the birth process and a sense of fulfillment. The baby's skin is so soft, we want to continually touch it. Cuddling, holding, and kissing the bundle of joy is a wonderful part of parenting. It feels right and good to protect a defenseless newborn. We want to care for this little miracle and plan for his or her future. Bonds and ties are formed in families of all kinds, colors, and cultures.

Yet, not everything that happens to us as children is good. In some cases, tragically bad things happen to us as we grow up in families. All marriages are not made in heaven. Some heavy tensions often accompany a man and woman saying, "I do." In other words, there are some things about any person we marry about which we might want to say, "I don't" instead of "I do." What about work schedules at home and in the workplace? What about tensions related to how to spend or save money? What about budgets, car payments, or when and how often to visit relatives? What about adjusting to differing expectations about sex from your marriage partner? The joys and fulfillment of love expressed for a new marriage partner abound, but stress waits at every corner of marriage relationships.

The birth of a baby is not without its problems, adjustments, and conflicts. Who gets how much attention from whom? Who doesn't get exhausted with the overload of the new work (as well as the old) that needs to be done? Who changes the diapers? What about new financial responsibilities on top of the old ones? These are just a few of the potential areas of stress and conflict.

As the child grows, problems pile up and multiply. The ecstasy of the birth often gives way to agony and drudgery. Needs and demands of the child are compounded when the child insists on being the center of family life. And those teen years can be a challenge, even in the best of families.

How about the agony and ecstasy of the relationships between brothers and sisters? Often brothers and/or sisters have great relationships but sometimes they are far from great. Sometimes sibling rivalry becomes sibling aggression, even sibling bullying. Misunderstandings are frequently recorded in the mind of siblings and remembered and played over and over again in the windmill of our minds until they break forth in angry words at strange, inopportune, and unguarded moments. We wish we could take those bitter words back, but they can't be retrieved. They are out there, ready to sting us back at some moment when we least expect them. Some siblings have an abundance of wonderful bonds of love, some have less. Some have few. Some, none.

Hurts can multiply because of what and how something is said. Misunderstandings can and do abound in every family. Occasionally misunderstandings are resolved, sometimes they are just tolerated, ready to raise their ugly heads when least expected. Frequently hurts just simmer, ready to pounce like a beast. Resentments can multiply like a communicable disease. And when someone dies, look out! Both the best and worst in families are revealed. Permanent good-byes are sometimes spoken.

The reasons for resentments in Jesus' family are different from those in our families, but they are there, as we see in our text.

According to the NRSV of the New Testament, our story begins with these poignant words: "Then he went home." The NIV translates the Greek original: "Then Jesus entered a house." The Phillips paraphrase simply says: "He went indoors." The context in all three translations clearly shows that it was family time as well as ministry time when Jesus came to the territory where he grew up and worked as a carpenter.

After his miraculous birth in Bethlehem, Jesus was circumcised in Jerusalem and taken by his family to Egypt until King Herod died. Then the family returned to Galilee, where they believed there would be less danger than in the city of Jerusalem. Whether Jesus went to the home where he was raised and worked, to a neighbor's house in Nazareth, or just into a house in the area of his hometown is incidental to our story. The point Mark's gospel makes is that Jesus was somewhere near where family and longtime friends lived and trouble was about to burst forth.

After a sojourn into Egypt to avoid trouble, conflict, and possible death, Joseph and Mary had settled in the territory of Galilee, in the town of Nazareth. Except for the one incident when Jesus was twelve and went to Jerusalem with his family for Passover, we know nothing about him until he was thirty years old and announced that he was called by God to leave home and declare the good news of God. In addition, Jesus declared kingdom of God people, who did God's will, to be his new family.

Conflict was not new to Jesus. Since sons usually followed the vocation of their fathers, it is likely that Jesus was a carpenter in Joseph's shop and as the oldest son took over the carpentry business when his father died. Then Jesus announced that he was going off to be an itinerant preacher. It isn't going overboard to suppose that one of the family member said, "And who is going to take care the family business when you are off preaching?" Nor would it be beyond reason to guess that some member of the family raised this question, "Just who is going to take care of us?" or "Aren't you being irresponsible by running off this way? Who's going to take care of your mother if you don't?" "What kind of son are you?" "Don't you care?" Conflict arose.

When Jesus said, "good-bye," to his family and friends in Nazareth, at best there must have been a lot of confusion. At worst, a fuse called bitterness was lit in the hearts of family members and neighbors which gave rise to resentment, criticism, and eventually an explosive decision to "take charge of him (Jesus) because they said, 'He is out of his mind' " (Mark 3:21). Trouble was brewing. Conflict.

At the moment Jesus returned to his home territory, his family came to seize him and try to get him out of danger from the religious and secular powers who were objecting to Jesus' words and deeds. Jesus' family was concerned about what Jesus was doing and what people were saying about him. Some were saying that Jesus was a miracle man. Others were saying he was a dangerous enemy. Some family members were thinking, "Jesus has gone way overboard. He's acting in crazy ways. Maybe he'll come to his senses and come home with us and settle down to a normal life as the head of Joseph's family and business."

The initial thoughts of the family members who came to take charge of Jesus were multiplied many times over when Jesus refused to see them, saying, "... My mother, my brothers and my sisters want to see me? My family members are really those who do God's will" (my paraphrase of Mark 3:34-35). In other words, "My new family is called 'kingdom of God people,'" those who do God's will.

The gospel of Matthew (10:36) reports Jesus saying, "A man's enemies will be members of his own household." Mark shows the truth of this saying in Jesus' own family. He reports the challenging and seemingly harsh words of Jesus that his real family is not those to whom he is physically linked, but those with whom he is spiritually bound, those who do God's will.

According to Luke's gospel, the mother of Jesus was acutely aware that this moment was coming. Mary had heard the prediction of Simeon, the old man in the temple at Jesus' circumcision, that "this child is destined for the falling and rising of many in Israel and to be a sign that will be spoken against, so that the thoughts of many hearers will be revealed. And a sword will pierce your own soul too." At this moment when Jesus refused to see his own family and spoke of family in such different terms than they had ever heard, Mary must have felt the prick of that sword beginning to stab her. It was a harsh and hurtful good-bye time.

41

Jesus' brothers and sisters must have felt the tip of the sword beginning to pierce their hearts too. They must have thought Jesus had become an uncontrollable religious fanatic, a family embarrassment, a scandal that must somehow be handled. The Barclay translation of Mark 3:21 is "he has taken leave of his senses." The NRSV simply says, "He has gone out of his mind."

His family could see that Jesus was headed for serious trouble. Why didn't he see it? He was taking unnecessary and dangerous risks. Why would he do that? His family thought there was only one explanation. Jesus was somehow just not himself. He must be saved from self-destruction. No sensible and sane man would have opposed the powers of the Orthodox religious leaders of the day. Jesus opposed them. He was having a head-on collision with them. His family went to the house where Jesus was teaching, seeking to stop the disaster which was about to go from bad to worse. No one could take on the scribes, Pharisees, and other religious leaders of the day and survive the confrontation. Jesus took them on. He must be saved from destroying himself.

The family must have felt that Jesus had thrown away his former friendships in Nazareth. They must have felt that Jesus was respected in that community and now he had made other friends of suspicious fishermen, a reformed tax-collector, and a fanatical political zealot, among other shady characters. That worried the family. That conflicted them.

The family must have felt that Jesus had thrown away security. He had had a job and an income. He had had some material goods and respect in his hometown of Nazareth. He could have settled down, gotten married, and raised a family. Instead, he launched out on a journey to disaster. Someone had to save him while there was still time.

The family must have thought that Jesus had thrown away safety. Jesus launched out into ministry that was so risky that it would surely get him hurt or maybe killed. Jesus was choosing a path of certain failure. Someone had to rescue him.

The family had to have been sure that Jesus had thrown away common sense. He was indifferent to the reputation he was getting. He didn't seem to care what people were saying about him. Crowds came in great numbers to hear him but the religious leaders opposed him and they said so. He appeared to be a fanatic who had "gone off the deep end." The family concluded that he must be saved from himself. "He must be out of his mind," they said. Someone had to take care of him. It appeared he couldn't take care of himself.

Then it got worse.

The family's worst fears were realized when Jesus refused to see them. Someone told Jesus that his mother and brothers and sisters were present and wanted to see him. He answered the inquiry with a question: "Who are my mother and my brothers and my sisters?" Then Jesus answered his own question. "Whoever does God's will is my brother and sister and mother" (Mark 3:35).

Challenging words. Words of conflict. Words of determination. Words of division. Words of "good-bye."

He had just said, "If a house is divided against himself, it can't stand" (Mark 3:25). Now, he seemed to be dividing his own house, saying "good-bye" to his physical family in favor of a new spiritual family of those who followed God's will.

Jesus was saying that real kinship is not primarily a matter of flesh and blood but the ties that come from a common desire to follow the will of God. Real kinship comes from a common goal with people in God's faith family, whether or not they are blood relatives. Real kinship is not anti-physical family, just above-and-beyond-physical family. Real kinship is in the family of believers, the kingdom of God people.

As far as we know, Jesus' family didn't get to see him that day. That's the bad news. But the good news is that later, after Jesus was crucified and resurrected, his brother James became head of the church in Jerusalem and at a critical time Luke mentions an amazing turnaround that took place after Jesus ascended into heaven. Along with other true disciples, Mary, the mother of Jesus, and Jesus' brothers, joined in the upper room for prayer (Acts 1:12-14). Faith in the risen and ascended Jesus Christ, the Lord and Savior of all, became the ultimate tie that bound Jesus' physical family, and all believers, to God as well as to one another in the family of God.

Proper 6
Pentecost 3
Ordinary Time 11
Mark 4:26-34

He also said, "The kingdom of God is as if someone would scatter seed on the ground, and would sleep and rise night and day, and the seed would sprout and grow, he does not know how. The earth produces of itself, first the stalk, then the head, then the full grain in the head. But when the grain is ripe, at once he goes in with his sickle, because the harvest has come." He also said, "With what can we compare the kingdom of God, or what parable will we use for it? It is like a mustard seed, which, when sown upon the ground, is the smallest of all the seeds on earth; yet when it is sown it grows up and becomes the greatest of all shrubs, and puts forth large branches, so that the birds of the air can make nests in its shade." With many such parables he spoke the word to them, as they were able to hear it; he did not speak to them except in parables, but he explained everything in private to his disciples.

Some Things I've Learned
Since I Knew It All

Have you ever suffered from "sophomoritis"? It's not a physical disease, like arthritis. It's a spiritual disease many college sophomores get when they get filled up with knowledge, come home on a vacation, and act like they know more than the folks around whom they grew up, especially their parents and younger siblings. That happened to a young man named Adam. He was studying to be an engineer at the University of Illinois in Urbana. On Christmas break, he got quite caught up with himself and started acting as if he had much more knowledge than his family. He excused them, of course, because his family members had never been to college, but he was quite sure that his father just didn't know much about anything and his mother knew even less. As for his younger brother and sister, well, it wasn't even worth the time of day to talk to them. When Adam talked, it was with an air of superiority.

His family noticed the change in his behavior right away, it even caused a few squabbles with his younger brother. When Adam left to go back to college, his father explained to the others, "Many students go through that kind of thing. As they begin to learn new things, they think they know a lot. When they learn a lot more, they know that they don't know very much. The truly smart person knows that there is so much more to learn in his field that he really is humbled by what he *doesn't* know."

Adam had not only been critical of his family for what he considered their lack of knowledge, but he had also been critical of their average lifestyle and their common house and car. "When I get out of college, I'll make a big salary, drive a big car, and own a big, beautiful house," he boasted to Betty Lou, his younger sister.

"Is bigger better?" Betty Lou asked.

"Always," Adam replied crisply and loudly. "Big is what life is all about."

Adam lived that creed, "Big is better and bigger is better yet." After college, he became a big success. He had three luxury cars and a house three times the size of his father's house. He often tried to tell his dad how happy he was and how much money he had. His father, Joshua, always told him to remember what he had learned about Jesus as a boy in Sunday school, church, and home. For most of his adult life, Adam neglected God, the teachings of Jesus, and the biblical base that his parents had given him for life. Instead, his creed, "More, more, more; the bigger the better," resulted in values that led him further and further from the values he had been taught as a youngster. "I can be a good guy without God," he said. He was only fooling himself, but he wouldn't listen to anyone else.

The biblical corrective for such attitudes and boasts, and for any and all aspects of an attitude of superiority, is this little parable spoken by our Lord and presented to us in Mark 4:26-34. We know people like Adam who go through phases when they act like they are superior, often to cover up feelings of inferiority. We also know that temptations and the demons of bragging, putting other people down, and thinking that we are bigger and better than others, lurk just beneath the surface in all of us. In other words, all of us need to hear this biblical corrective for pride, arrogance, and the dangers of being self-centered. That's why we need to hear what Jesus says about the kingdom of God, the biggest and smallest thing of all. "It (the kingdom of God) is like a mustard seed..." (Mark 4:30).

Is the kingdom of God just another technical term used by theologians and pastors, like lawyers use big legal terms, doctors use complicated medical and drug terms, and government people use confusing tax jargon? No, it isn't. As we listen to Jesus speak of the kingdom of God, keep in mind that he is telling us what God is like, what we are like, and what our neighbors are like.

As Jesus used the term "the kingdom of God," it means that God reigns over us for our own good. That God reigns over our lives is the biggest thing of all.

God rules. Not dictators, not kings or government officials, not bullies, arrogant bosses or relatives, but God. We don't rule our own lives. God rules the universe, including you and me. That's why we pray, "Thy will be done on earth as it is in heaven."

God rules over us. Whether we believe it or not, whether we like it or not, whether it is acceptable to us or not, God rules over us. The Bible teaches that we are ultimately responsible to and will stand before God who judges the living and the dead. That's why we pray, "Thy kingdom come."

God rules over us for our own good. God doesn't rule because he needs to feel powerful or have people bow before him. He rules over us because he knows what is best for us. He will lead us to what is beneficial for us if we don't refuse to follow his ways. That's why we pray, "Lead us not into temptation, but deliver us from evil," or as another translation puts it, "Save us from the great ordeal (the ultimate suffering of God being silent) and deliver us from the evil one."[1]

Life is a mystery. An avid reader once said, "I always

read the last lines of a mystery story before I read the story." When asked why, she said, "I want to know how the mystery is going to end before I begin it." As Christians, we know how the mystery of life will end. At the end of time, as Paul says, "... Every knee will bow... and every tongue confess that Jesus is Lord to the glory of God the Father" (Philippians 2:9-11). Since that is true, we know how we are called to live, under the reign or rule of God for our own good.

All of us sin and get caught in the trap of being self-centered. The center of the word "sin" is "I." That's the unsolvable human problem. No act of the self can lift the self out of the self by the self because the self is the problem. We need to be saved. We need a Savior.

Adam, lived life with the big "I" in the middle. He claimed that he didn't need a Savior. He tried to rule other people and run his own life without any reference to his Creator or Redeemer. He paid no attention to the Holy Spirit who was available to bring him spiritual growth and fulfillment. Adam thought that bigger is always better, so he tried to get more and more things of the world.

On the back of his big, beautiful motor home he placed a bumper sticker that read: "At the end, the one with the most toys wins." On the back bumper of one of his big, beautiful sport cars he had another bumper sticker: "Number one drives here."

Adam's father warned him that he was flirting with disaster, but he paid no attention. His dad had frequently said, "Unless that which is above you, controls that which is within you, that which is around you, will. Idolatry has consequences." Adam didn't like that, so he tuned out his dad's words. "I don't believe in God anymore," he said. "I don't need God." Adam had money and power. He thought he had it all. He thought he knew it all. Troubles waited around the corner.

Adam's life seemed to go well enough, but something was out of kilter and trouble was on the horizon. After five years of marriage with many ups and downs, Adam's wife divorced him and the divorce was expensive. The tension between the former husband and wife got worse as years passed. When his two children grew into teenagers, Adam found that they avoided him. His attitude of always saying that he was right drove a wedge between him and his children. Former friends were alienated by his tendency to blame everyone but himself for his troubles. Adam's troubles compounded when his self-righteous attitude caused him to get fired at work.

Adam's parents, his brother, and his sister tried to help but were frustrated since he continually refused to take responsibility for his troubles. On top of all his other troubles, Adam had a drinking problem. He maintained he wasn't an alcoholic and that he could stop drinking any time he chose to, but somehow the drinking never stopped. He was locked into the alcoholic syndrome — drinking to solve problems until drinking became his biggest problem which he tried to solve by drinking. One drink was too much and a thousand drinks were not enough — the alcoholic predicament.

Adam's predicament was compounded by his attitude. "Me first" is a self-defeating creed which precludes hearing the still small voice of God. Looking for the big, expensive, and powerful things in life, life's illusions, Adam missed the biggest thing of all, God's kingdom.

Duane "Bud" Potter was the leader of a small men's Bible study group. The men had a great time studying God's word, but Bud and others knew they should do more than study. "We need to be action oriented. We need to do some work with our hands, as well as with our heads," Bud said. "We are just beginning to line up the projects, but we want to select a name." The group turned to their pastor.

"Why don't you call yourselves 'Go and Do Likewise,' after the parable of the Good Samaritan" (Luke 10:3), the pastor responded. The men's group began their service of "going and doing likewise," by painting houses for people. They painted for people who could not afford to hire someone to do that work. These people also couldn't afford to buy the paint. The "Go and Do Likewise" men bought the paint and did the work with no charge. The people in the community who received the work found it hard to believe that anyone was doing that kind of work for them for no payment at all. They were amazed when Bud and his friends told them that they were just doing what Jesus said to do. "You Christians are amazing," many said.

Over 100 houses later, the "Go and Do Likewise" (GADL) movement moved from a small community effort to an international ministry. Bud heard from a pastor in a small village in Africa that he and his small congregation needed help. Today, Bud and the men, women, and youth GADL workers have made many trips to that small village in Kenya, West Africa, where clean water, new buildings, and education for children are now real.[2]

From the small world of a twelve-man Bible study to an international movement — that's what could be called the fulfillment of both the mustard seed parable and the parable of the Good Samaritan. That ministry movement has the opposite foundation than the creed on which Adam had built his life. A life lived for God and others — that's a contrast to the "me, me, me," philosophy of Adam.

Jesus said, "The kingdom of God is as if someone would scatter seed on the ground" (Mark 4:26). Then he added, "It (the kingdom of God) is like a mustard seed which is the smallest seed you plant in the ground..." (Mark 4:31). In both cases Jesus is telling us that small beginnings, when linked to God's purposes, can have enormous results.

The high, holy kingdom of God that is the biggest and most powerful thing imaginable, is also a small, small world of unseen spiritual forces for good that grow imperceptibly. Count on it. Drop seeds by witnessing for God and you will find that God can use them to change people and turn people back to him. Mustard seeds can grow into great trees.

The farmer doesn't make his seed grow. Neither does the Christian witness make his spiritual seeds grow. If spiritual seeds grow to a mighty size, like "Go and Do Likewise," it is God who brings the growth. God's witnesses don't convert anyone. They are just used by God to begin the process of growth by words and deeds. Bud puts it this way, "It is God who gets the credit for the good works done by 'Go and Do Likewise'; not me and not our group. Jesus gets the glory, not us."

Night and day spiritual growth can take place "underground" in quiet out of the way places — small towns, small churches, by softly spoken words of affirmation as well as by loud brass bands, huge choirs, and dynamic eloquent preachers in cathedrals. The parable of the mustard seed encourages us to believe that small deposits can result in large growth — in us and in those we serve. Often, we don't even know that the seeds we planted are growing in another person's heart.

At his father's funeral, Adam asked if he might be one of the family members who said a few words. Some family members shuddered at the thought, fearful that Adam might make a fool of himself. After all, as far as anyone knew his life had gone from bad to worse. Adam might spoil the funeral for those who had come to honor and remember his dad. But since he was the son, there was no way to keep him from fulfilling his request.

When his turn came, Adam walked to the podium and tried to smile through his tears.

Dad always told me to love God and serve people. He not only told me that, he also lived by that creed. Dad was the smartest man I ever met. Of course, as some of you know, I haven't always followed his ways or his example. As a matter of fact, for much of my life, I've gone in the opposite direction from my father's ways. For a season of my life I thought my dad didn't know much of anything about how life really worked. For that season I have deep regrets. I was a "know-it-all" who didn't know much of anything. I was all puffed up with myself.

As Dad predicted, life came tumbling in on me with my divorce, my self-pity, the loss of my job, and a problem with drinking that I mistakenly thought I could handle, but which I continually messed up. The hardships and hard knocks of life often teach us some things we can never learn in school. One of the things I've learned since my sophomore year in college when I thought I knew it all is that small, quiet beginnings can often lead to great achievements.

Small, quiet beginnings and consistent faith in God with selfless service to others — that's what my father was all about. That's what I want to be about. About a year ago I began a turnaround in my life that centers on God. I joined Alcoholics Anonymous, started attending church again, and joined a small men's group that studies the Bible and does service for others. It is called, "Go and Do Likewise." I know that this is just a beginning and daily I pray that I will not fall back into a life of self-centered behavior, but I now believe in small beginnings. Finally, I am following my father's advice. Dad always said, "Son, if you just remember that Jesus is your Lord and Savior and that he wants you to serve others, you'll do well in life." That's the most important thing I've learned since I thought I knew it all.

Adam's mother and sister were sitting in the first pew in front of the podium, smiling through their tears.

The ads often tell us that big is always better than small, that bigger is even better than big, and huge is better than all. That's an illusion perpetrated by those who just want to make more money by selling us more and more stuff. Sometimes, when it comes to really important things, like coming back to God, it takes parents, Sunday school teachers, and other seemingly unimportant witnesses who plant seeds that may be hidden for years, but eventually bear fruit.

The world says that small is of little value. In fact, small beginnings in the kingdom of God can lead to the biggest thing of all — eternal life.

---

1. Ron Lavin, *Abba (Another Look at The Lord's Prayer)* (Lima, Ohio: CSS Publishing Company, 2003), pp. 69ff.

2. Further information on "Go and Do Likewise" can be found by contacting Bud Potter at dolikewise@aol.com.

Proper 7
Pentecost 4
Ordinary Time 12
Mark 4:35-41

On that day, when evening had come, he said to them, "Let us go across to the other side." And leaving the crowd behind, they took him with them in the boat, just as he was. Other boats were with him. A great windstorm arose, and the waves beat into the boat, so that the boat was already being swamped. But he was in the stern, asleep on the cushion; and they woke him up and said to him, "Teacher, do you not care that we are perishing?" He woke up and rebuked the wind, and said to the sea, "Peace! Be still!" Then the wind ceased, and there was a dead calm. He said to them, "Why are you afraid? Have you still no faith?" And they were filled with great awe and said to one another, "Who then is this, that even the wind and the sea obey him?"

Close Calls

Have you ever had a close call? Have you ever been in an accident where you almost died? Have you ever been overwhelmed by an event or loss so great that you wondered how you would ever get through it? When a close call came, have you ever felt that God either didn't care or that he was asleep because you couldn't reach him?

That is what is going on in our story, the story of the apostles in a little boat during a violent storm on a lake called Galilee where the wind rushes down from the hills with such velocity that even seasoned fishermen are sure they are going to die. This storm is called a "furious squall" in the NIV of the New Testament. The NRSV simply calls it "a great wind storm." Whatever you call it, it was one of those moments the men who experienced it would call a near-death experience, a close call.

The Jones family moved to a new house in south Florida near a pond. There were two other houses on the pond, one owned by a doctor. One day, shortly after they moved in, the Jones' three children went swimming in the pond. Suddenly, out of nowhere a 400-pound alligator appeared. The doctor happened to be out and saw the alligator. He yelled to the children. Two of them heard the cry and headed for shore. The third child, Mike, was under the water using his diving gear to look beneath the surface. The other two children got near the shore, looked back, and saw the alligator bearing down like a torpedo on their brother. One of them started back to warn Mike, but it was too late.

The alligator was upon the boy. He was about to swallow him whole, but when the alligator chomped down on the boy's head, he found the diving gear distasteful and spit him out.

Mike swam as fast as he could underwater toward the shore. The alligator swam round and round in circles trying to find the boy. When Mike surfaced, the alligator located him and headed toward him again. Mike was about twenty feet from shore when the alligator caught him, this time by the feet.

By this time, Mike's mother, who was on shore, had waded out to where the boy was. She grabbed his extended hands and started to pull. It was a 400-pound alligator pulling in one direction and a 100-pound mother pulling in the other. The flippers, which were distasteful to the alligator, caused him to let go. The determined mother won the tug-of-war.

Today, Mike's only evidence of the horrifying event is scars on his head and feet from the alligator bites and scars on his wrists where his mother's nails had dug in when she pulled him to safety. "That close call gave us a new perspective on life and God," Mike's mother said. "At first we doubted God, but now we have reordered our priorities; we've gone back to church and put the Lord first."

Most of us don't experience close calls that extreme, but we know what close calls are. Life has a way of dishing out close calls of one kind or another and yes, when that happens, even the best Christians at first may ask: "Does God even care?" Later, we may get the big picture.

Our story leads us into the deep waters of two life-changing questions: *Is the Lord asleep when we need him most?* and *Who is in charge here?*

That's what the apostles thought and said to one another

on the storm tossed waves of the Lake of Galilee. In fact, as the waves broke over the boat and nearly swamped it, the exhausted Jesus was sleeping in the stern. The frightened apostles, some of them fisherman by trade, woke Jesus with a question, "Teacher, don't you care if we drown?" We can identify with the disciples. That's how it feels sometimes when life comes tumbling in, when the storms of life threaten to take our life away, when the God we love and have followed suddenly seems to go silent when we need him most.

In his book *The Silence of God* Helmut Thielicke tells of times like these in his life, especially during World War II, when the terrible physical suffering of war-torn people were further complicated by what at times seemed like God's silence. Thielicke suggests that John the Baptist had thoughts about the silence of Jesus when he was in prison, just before he died.

> How long do you keep us in suspense? Tell us freely whether you are the Christ. Call down from heaven that you are. Do you not see how dreadful are the effects of your silence? Do you not see how much more merciful it would be if this voice were to ring out so that all would have to hear it... Why do you not make things clear, God?[1]

The apostles were perishing and Jesus lay there sleeping, silent. They knew he cared. They had experienced his care. They had seen his care for the needy. But they felt at that moment like he didn't care. If he cared, wouldn't he be awake and doing something to save them? Have you ever felt that way? Many Christians, even the most faithful, have gone through this midnight of the soul.

Thielicke describes it this way: "How many meaningless blows of fate there seem to be! — life, suffering, injustice, death, massacres, destruction; and all under a silent heaven which apparently has nothing to say."[2] Martin Luther knew the meaning of the silence of God. He called it *anfectugen*, a claustrophobic feeling of being suffocated and seemingly having no way out.

All of these feelings about heavenly silence are summarized by the apostles' question, "Don't you care?" It is a moment of desperation for them and us. We want an answer. We must have an answer. We demand an answer.

Jesus gave an answer. In part, it is an answer we hoped for, but part of the answer, the part we might call "the reversal," we do not expect.

Jesus got up from his sleep, rebuked the wind and spoke to the waves with authority like the apostles had never seen before. "Be still," Jesus said, and the wind and waves obeyed him. That's what we hoped would happen. Because we've heard the story before, that's what we expect to happen. But this massive word from Jesus to the elements must not be taken for granted. It is astounding. It is shocking that nature obeyed Jesus. Nature is his to command.

Jesus, the great I Am, is telling his obedient servants, nature's elements, what to do. Amazing — staggering — moving — no wonder the apostles asked, "Who is this? Even the wind and waves obey him!" Here Jesus as Lord commands the forces of nature, like so many puppy dogs.

The surprising part of the story is the questions and the meaning of the questions Jesus asked. "Why are you afraid? Do you still have no faith?" Who wouldn't be afraid in a storm like that? Who wouldn't fear for their lives? Who wouldn't scream at the heavens for help and receiving none, feel deserted? What do you mean, Jesus, by your question about faith? We have faith, but this is a life-threatening emergency. We haven't lost faith, we are just scared to death.

What do these questions of our Lord mean? Of course, there is the basic meaning. To have faith in God means to trust him in the worst times as well as the best times. Faith means when you get to the end of your rope, you tie a knot and hang on, even in those times when God seems silent like when Jesus cried out from the cross, "My God, my God, why have you forsaken me?" Yes, but there is more, much more, in these questions than at first meets the eye or comes to mind.

Consider that the Bible was written by Jews. Consider that Jesus was a Jew. What is going on in this and many similar Bible stories can best be understood if we allow ourselves to get into Hebrew thinking. In Hebrew thinking, the one who asks the question, not the one who answers the question, is in charge.

When Jesus was asked a question about paying taxes, he answered by asking, "Whose image is on this coin?" When Jesus was asked about his origins, he replied, "I will answer your question if you answer this one: 'Was John the Baptist sent by God or not?' " When a lawyer asked Jesus, "Who is my neighbor?" Jesus never answered his question. Instead Jesus left a question hanging in the air for the lawyer to consider: "Are you going to be a neighbor to those in need or not?"

A Jew was once asked, "Why do you Jews always answer questions with questions?" He replied, "Why not?"

In Jewish thinking, the one who asks the question is in charge. A dramatic shift in the meaning of our story takes place when we move from the questions of the apostles, "Are you asleep? Don't you care?" to the questions of Jesus, "Why are you afraid? Do you still have no faith?" In fact, a reversal takes place. The reversal is described in these words: "You are not in charge here. I am."

The bind in our story of the little boat in a really big storm is the human tendency to think there is no option to our being in charge. We ask questions about life and death as if we are in charge. The reversal, indeed the good news in our story, is that in fact God is in charge. He just seems to be sleeping. He cares for us more than we will ever know. To see what I mean, consider interpreting this scripture story with another scripture story.

Consider the story of Job, in many respects, a parallel story to the apostles in an unstable little boat in chaotic waters. Generally speaking, Job is a prototype of unjust suffering. After all, he was a good man, trying to follow God in every way. Then *whoosh*, like a storm, life came tumbling in on his head. A man of God doing his duty should be rewarded with blessings on blessings, right? But as we know from the story of Job and from our own lives, it doesn't always happen that way. As a matter of fact, the best believers often suffer the most. What's going on here in the story of Job? What's going on in life in your story and mine? Life just doesn't seem fair at times.

Job was tending his farm, taking care of his family, praying regularly, and following God's ways when along came tragedy after tragedy. His crops failed, his health broke, his children died. Then as if to add insult to injury, Job's wife turned against him with biting criticism. His friends insisted that he was being punished for his sins. With friends like that, who needs enemies?

The multiplication of troubles and tribulations caused Job to do what we do. He started to turn his resentment about his situation into speculation and accusation against God. "Why me? Am I being punished for something I've done? God, are you asleep or is it that you just don't care?" Sound familiar? Projection — blaming others and eventually blaming God for our troubles — is an all too familiar human reaction when life comes tumbling in and we don't know what else to do. Like Job, we dump on God.

In the story of Job, the reversal came when God answered Job's questions with his own questions. God introduces his questions with a stunning declaration: "Stand up now, like a man and answer the questions I ask you," said the Lord (Job 38:1, 3 TEV). Then the questions put Job's situation into a different light:

"Where were you when I made the world?"
"Who decided how large it would be?"
"Do you know all the answers?"
"Who closed the gates to hold back the sea?"
"Have you ever in all your life commanded a day to dawn?"
(Job 38:4-5, 8, 12 paraphrased)

We are at the turning point in the story. The turning point is that God is asking the questions. Since this is a Jewish story, that means God is in charge, not man. God is in the middle, not man.

In modern life, we have the tendency to think of ourselves as being central. The elevation of man to the middle to replace God in the middle has been a tendency from the beginning of time, but it got a big boost in the Renaissance when art and science began to replace religion as the central theme for intellectuals, then for the masses. Man in the middle, trying to control everything, being critical of everything, evaluating everything, being first, last, and always central in his own thinking — that's the bind in which we find ourselves today. We can't get ourselves out of our own hands.

No act of the self can lift the self out of the self by the self because too much self is the biggest problem we have. The story of Job in the Old Testament and the story of the apostles on the stormy sea in the New Testament are both biblical correctives for our tendency to think of ourselves as the ones in control of life. When Job calmed down and listened to God's questions and when the apostles observed the calm sea around them, they were astonished to discover who they were really dealing with — the Lord of heaven and earth. That is what brought peace of mind and soul to them. That is what can bring peace of mind and soul to us today.

When Saint Paul wrote, "From now on... we regard no one from a human point of view" (2 Corinthians 5:16), he was making this same point. The human point of view of people and situations is too limited. Saint Paul had discovered the ability to get up high, high enough to see from a heavenly perspective what most people miss — God's perspective on how things really are. That's what the story of Job and the story of the storm on the Sea of Galilee are all about.

Saint Augustine put it this way in a prayer: "Watch over us who are still on this dangerous voyage. Frail is our vessel, and the ocean wide, but in your mercy you have set our course."

If you have ever had a close call, perhaps the biblical corrective for thinking too highly of yourself has dawned on you too — like it dawned on Augustine, Paul, Job, the apostles, and thousands of others. If it hasn't dawned on you yet, maybe it will soon.

---

1. Helmut Thielicke, *The Silence of God* (Grand Rapids: William Eerdmans Publishing, 1962), p. 13.

2. *Ibid.*, p. 14.

*When Jesus had crossed again in the boat to the other side,
a great crowd gathered around him; and he was by the
sea. Then one of the leaders of the synagogue named Jairus
came and, when he saw him, fell at his feet and begged him
repeatedly, "My little daughter is at the point of death. Come
and lay your hands on her, so that she may be made well,
and live." So he went with him. And a large crowd followed
him and pressed in on him. Now there was a woman who
had been suffering from hemorrhages for twelve years. She
had endured much under many physicians, and had spent
all that she had; and she was no better, but rather grew
worse. She had heard about Jesus, and came up behind
him in the crowd and touched his cloak, for she said, "If
I but touch his clothes, I will be made well." Immediately
her hemorrhage stopped; and she felt in her body that she
was healed of her disease. Immediately aware that power
had gone forth from him, Jesus turned about in the crowd
and said, "Who touched my clothes?" And his disciples said
to him, "You see the crowd pressing in on you; how can you
say, 'Who touched me?'" He looked all around to see who
had done it. But the woman, knowing what had happened to
her, came in fear and trembling, fell down before him, and
told him the whole truth. He said to her, "Daughter, your
faith has made you well; go in peace, and be healed of your
disease." While he was still speaking, some people came
from the leader's house to say, "Your daughter is dead. Why
trouble the teacher any further?" But overhearing what they
said, Jesus said to the leader of the synagogue, "Do not fear,
only believe." He allowed no one to follow him except Peter,*

James, and John, the brother of James. When they came to the house of the leader of the synagogue, he saw a commotion, people weeping and wailing loudly. When he had entered, he said to them, "Why do you make a commotion and weep? The child is not dead but sleeping." And they laughed at him. Then he put them all outside, and took the child's father and mother and those who were with him, and went in where the child was. He took her by the hand and said to her, "Talitha cum," which means, "Little girl, get up!" And immediately the girl got up and began to walk about (she was twelve years of age). At this they were overcome with amazement. He strictly ordered them that no one should know this, and told them to give her something to eat.

So, You Want to Get Well?

There are four stories going on in this text: 1) the story of a humble leader, 2) the story of a sick woman, 3) the story of a dead little girl, and 4) your story and mine.

We want to be sure to get at the truth of the Bible stories, but we also need to look at the personal connection, the application of the text to our lives. That's your story and mine. In other words, preaching Bible stories must not only be true to the text; preaching also must make a difference. This text about Jesus' healing power is true; it also makes a difference in our lives.

The presenting problem, the "itch" for which Jesus provides the "scratch" is a request from a synagogue leader named Jairus. This point of departure is the plea of this community leader for Jesus to come to his home and heal his dying daughter.

Jairus urgently requested that Jesus help his child. He didn't just ask; he begged the Lord to do something that no one else had been able to do — to bring the young girl from the brink of death back to life. We feel the tragedy in the plea.

The plea touches the soul. When a child is sick or hurting, we get worried. When he/she is very sick, we get very worried. And when a child is sick unto death, we get worried to death. As one father put it, "I'd rather die myself than have my little girl die." And he meant it. The presenting problem draws us into the story. We feel the pain of the father.

The father was an important man, a person of considerable influence, a synagogue ruler. In Jesus' time, a synagogue ruler was the president of a board of elders for a worship and education center for the Jewish community. He was a respected leader in the community, the one who decided who would preach and teach in the synagogue. He also made sure that the house of God was kept clean, repaired, and ready for worship of the almighty. The house of God had to have a sense of respect and great dignity. So did the man who was in charge of that synagogue.

This father had dignity, but whatever dignity he had was forgotten as he arrived where Jesus was teaching. Pride forgotten, Jairus fell to his knees like a beggar and humbly asked Jesus to come to his home and do something for his little girl. It isn't easy for a man of honor to bow his head, fall to his knees and beg, but nothing would interfere with this request. Nothing. He would do anything for his child. Do you feel that parental pulse beating as you hear and imagine the drama?

This father had responsibilities. The synagogue was the school for the community, the social center of town, and the place where devout Jews gathered for worship each Sabbath. Responsibilities aside, Jairus came to see the man about whom two things were being whispered and shouted among the Jews. Some said he was a dangerous agitator and revolutionary teacher who could not be trusted; others insisted Jesus was a healer sent from God and that he had restored many people of all ages to health. Jairus clung to the hope that Jesus would heal his child.

This father had hope. He set his fears aside. He had his mind focused on one thing: his little girl. If there was any chance that Jesus could restore her to health as he had done for others, Jairus wanted this for his child. If he was going to face criticism for associating with Jesus, so be it. If the

Pharisees and Sadducees were going to put pressure on the community to scorn him, that was of no account. If the elders would ask for his resignation, that was secondary. Healing was priority one.

That's how our text begins. Suddenly, as if out of nowhere, there is a major interruption. The quest of a desperate father for healing of his dying daughter is interrupted by the quest of a sick and desperate woman who has known one disappointment after another in her search for health.

The first story is pushed out of the way by a simple incident that from human standards should have been ignored. A simple, predictable incident is seemingly blown out of proportion when Jesus' asked: "Who touched me?"

One of the apostles, or another of Jesus' friends, gave the natural human reaction to that strange question: "What do you mean, 'Who touched me?' Can't you see the crowds all around you pushing and shoving to get close, bumping one another repeatedly and bumping you in the process? What's the problem? Someone touched you? So what?" Jesus never deals with this natural human response. He turned to the crowd with those deep, penetrating eyes that seemed to search the nooks and crannies of the human soul, and requested again with compassion in his eyes, "Who touched me?"

The crisis in the first story suddenly falls into second place as a strange, inferior-feeling, unnamed woman with a bleeding problem approached Jesus. Her problem had shamed her. Inconspicuously, slowly, hesitatingly, and meekly she appeared, then suddenly she was in a spotlight. Jesus searched her out. She looked back at the man looking right through the facade she erected. Feeling the healing of her body, forgetting the crowd, forgetting her embarrassment, forgetting herself, she fell at Jesus' feet. "I did it," she confessed like one who has sinned greatly. "I touched your robe."

Reaching down to touch the one who had touched his robe, Jesus said, "Daughter."

"Did he just call me daughter?" she must have thought. "What a tender way to speak. What will he say next?"

"Daughter, your faith has healed you. Go in peace and be freed from your suffering."

Here in this story of the befuddled, desperate, suffering woman we meet what might be called the courtesy of Christ. The woman's theology is totally unacceptable. She thinks that touching a piece of clothing will heal her. That's magic, not real faith. If she went to seminary, she would flunk out for practicing that kind of theology. But Jesus didn't see it that way. He leads us into a different way to see different people who are desperate for help. The compassion of Christ means that Jesus starts with people where they are. He doesn't say, as many seem to fear, "Get your theology in order, get your life fixed up before you come to me, and then I will talk with you." No, instead, surprisingly, he starts with us wherever we are and lifts us up higher if we just come to him, open and willing for him to do with us whatever he sees we need to have him do.

Like Jairus, who initiated the movement of this drama with the point of departure, the woman who was estranged from everyone by a massive, monstrous problem she didn't cause, and for which she could find no help, simply came as she was and did the best she could with what little she had. This nobody had tried everybody. No one had been able to help her. With stops and starts that would have discouraged almost anybody from trying again, she reached out once more. Maybe she didn't do it just right, but she did it — she reached out to Jesus in her own way, trying to remain inconspicuous. That's all that is necessary.

Thus this nobody, this bleeding outcast among the Jews[1], became a wise teacher of faith who announced to the world without words, "This man, this Jesus, is unlike anyone else who has ever lived. He will start with you wherever you are, just like he did with me. He changed my life. He can change yours." That is what is called a major reversal. Power had gone out from Jesus and into the broken woman. That is called a miraculous reversal.

The woman who wanted to get well, got more than she could ever have hoped for. More than her body was healed. Getting well meant that she was given a power of life she had never experienced before this encounter.

Suddenly, as we often see in the gospel of Mark, another interruption, a disrupting movement in the woman's story, comes bursting in. As Jesus was talking to the unnamed woman and healing her bleeding problem, some people came from Jairus' house with shocking news. "Your daughter is dead," they said. "Why bother the teacher anymore?" End of story. Hope canceled. Time to give up... wrong.

The story of the healing of Jairus' daughter is a story of dramatic contrasts. The story invites us to choose one side or the other. Despair or hope?

There is a dramatic contrast between the hopeless mourning of the people at Jairus' house and the quiet confident hope of Jesus. The mourning of the people who gathered around the little girl came from a feeling of despair. Despair goes beyond suffering. It is suffering without hope. The loud wailing of the people combined with the wailing of the flutes made for an atmosphere of unmanageable grief. What a shame... an unfulfilled life... a child who would never grow up... a mother and father with broken hearts... love lost and gone forever — or so it seemed to everyone there; everyone but Jesus.

Jesus saw beyond what seemed to be happening all the way to what was actually happening. He had the perspective of eternity and the power of God over death. Others saw only the misery of a pitiful child suffering and dying. Others saw only the tragedy. Jesus saw what God wanted to accomplish in that tragedy. When Jesus said, "The child is asleep," the people scorned him with ridicule and laughter. Jesus saw that the little girl could be awakened like it was time to get up in the morning. The people saw only the seemingly permanent sleep of the dead. That is a staggering contrast — opposite poles! Those are two different ways to think! The wailers and mourners saw misery, tragedy, and suffering. Jesus saw opportunity and hope. Choose — which side will you attach yourself to?

The wailers and mourners were caught in a demonic, un-restrained distress that is often present at the time of death. Jesus approached the little girl with a calmness and peace that was in dramatic contrast to all those around him. When they laughed at what they considered the apparent illusion of Jesus' comment about death being like sleeping from which someone could wake up, Jesus just kept walking straight toward his destination. Taking Peter, James, and John with him, he moved like one accustomed to winning. Jesus went directly to the little girl's bedroom. With tenderness and con-fidence, Jesus took the hand of the child and said, *"Talitha cum"* which means "Little girl, get up."

Jesus spoke in a Hebrew dialect called Aramaic, a com-mon language of the time. Peter, one of the three apostles who heard the words spoken, must have felt it was important to retain the calm serenity of the Aramaic words. When he retold the story to Mark, he retained the original Aramaic.

We are offered a choice in this dramatic story; a choice between the hysterical, out-of-control reaction of hopeless-ness in the face of death, or the serenity of Jesus who knows that for believers death is just a brief stopover on the way to freedom, a brief time before the fullness of the kingdom of God is ours.

These Bible stories are more than just interesting tales of old. They connect with your life and mine. They invite us to step into the middle of the drama and draw from them what God wants to say to us today. Do these ancient healing tales make a difference to you and me? Yes, I believe they do.

It may be helpful to keep the words of an old hymn before our mind's eyes as we think about how we are participants in these biblical dramas. The hymn "Just As I Am" is a reminder of how we come before God when we want to be healed. In addition to these two healing stories we have the assurance of the cross and resurrection of Jesus to add to our perspective, so we can sing, "Just as I am, without one plea, but that thy blood was shed for me... O Lamb of God, I come" (public domain). I come to be made well "just as I am." That's how the unnamed woman with the bleeding problem came. That's how the little girl came.

Just as I am, I come to Christ humbly, not proudly like one who has it all together, but humbly. If I come as a proud man before my Lord, that pride will get in the way of my healing. But if I come like Jairus, the unnamed woman, and the little girl, I will be open to what God has to give me. Healing of the body, healing of memories, and healing of broken spirits all begin by acknowledging that I am broken. As Luther once said, "It is God's nature to create out of nothing. If I am not nothing, God can't make anything out of me."

Just as I am, I come to Christ with appreciation and gratitude for what he does for me. There is no wellness without gratitude to God. Granger Westberg was a Lutheran pastor who spent his ministry connecting faith and health. He worked in medical schools as well as churches and seminaries. Some years ago, Granger lectured to doctors, nurses, and pastors at the University of Arizona School of Medicine. He asked a question: "What is the one thing, more than any other factor, that brings wellness to our lives?" There were many answers — all of them good answers, but wrong. After reviewing the importance of keeping in good physical shape, not eating wrong foods, not smoking, and a dozen other good answers, Westberg said, "According to a recent medical research project in which I was involved, it was discovered that the most important ingredient in health is gratitude. 'The attitude of gratitude,'" he said. To get well, it is essential that I come to God with an attitude of gratitude. Gratitude is the golden thread that runs through our story and the entire Bible.

O Lamb of God, I come with faith that you will care for my hurts. Whatever my hurts are, I need to lay them at the feet of Jesus. It may be that my hurts are physical, like the unnamed woman with blood issues. It may be that I come with hurts that are mental — resentments that I feel I have a right to feel because I have been so badly treated by someone.

O Lamb of God, I come sincerely giving up my self-pity and resentments. From a human point of view, I may have a right to them, but self-pity and resentments keep me sick. I may have a human "right" to them, but they are "rights" which are wrong for my own health and wellness. Resentments, like arteries, harden and have the same deadly result. A cousin to self-pity and resentments, an unwillingness to forgive may be "right" from a human point of view, but that unwillingness to forgive does much more damage to me, "the owner" than to the person against whom they are held, so I place them in your hands. Revenge too, O Lord, I turn over to you.

Granger Westberg asked the audience at the University of Arizona School of Medicine, "What is the one thing, more than any other single factor, that makes us sick? After many wrong answers, he told us that the medical research he and others had done showed that the single worst thing we can do if we want to be healthy is to be motivated by revenge. "Revenge causes more heart attacks, strokes, and other serious medical problems than any other factor," he said. When we come to Christ with our hurts, we had better also be willing to give up revenge against people who have sinned against us. If those who have hurt us are not willing to repent or make no effort to acknowledge what they have done wrong, they won't be forgiven; that's their problem. We have no control over that. We do have control over our willingness to forgive. That's why Jesus taught us to pray, "Forgive us our trespasses as we forgive those who trespass against us."

O Lamb of God, I come to you, sincerely seeking your help. Whatever my human condition, whether a physical problem or a problem in a relationship or any one of a hundred difficulties in which I may find myself, I come to you, Lord, knowing that I need help.

If I come, like the Pharisee in one of Jesus' parables saying, "I'm glad I'm not like this tax collector... I avoid sin, I go to church regularly, and say my prayers every night...." I will go away unforgiven. If, like the tax collector in that same parable, I say sincerely, "God be merciful to me, a sinner," I have opened the door to new life, health, and wellness.

O Lamb of God, I come to you without one plea, but that your blood was shed for me, I come; I come. I cannot carry my burdens and problems any longer. They are too heavy for me.

If you pray like that and like the unnamed woman in Jesus' story, you may hear the wonderful words: "Child of mine, your faith has made you well," or like the little girl, "Arise, my child, wake up from death."

1. Since the Jews of Jesus' time believed that blood was life, they spurned women during their periods and treated the bleeding woman in Mark like an outcast, almost like a leper.

Proper 9
Pentecost 6
Ordinary Time 14
Mark 6:1-13

He left that place and came to his hometown, and his disciples followed him. On the sabbath he began to teach in the synagogue, and many who heard him were astounded. They said, "Where did this man get all this? What is this wisdom that has been given to him? What deeds of power are being done by his hands! Is not this the carpenter, the son of Mary and brother of James and Joses and Judas and Simon, and are not his sisters here with us?" And they took offense at him. Then Jesus said to them, "Prophets are not without honor, except in their hometown, and among their own kin, and in their own house." And he could do no deed of power there, except that he laid his hands on a few sick people and cured them. And he was amazed at their unbelief. Then he went about among the villages teaching. He called the twelve and began to send them out two by two, and gave them authority over the unclean spirits. He ordered them to take nothing for their journey except a staff; no bread, no bag, no money in their belts; but to wear sandals and not to put on two tunics. He said to them, "Wherever you enter a house, stay there until you leave the place. If any place will not welcome you and they refuse to hear you, as you leave, shake off the dust that is on your feet as a testimony against them." So they went out and proclaimed that all should repent. They cast out many demons, and anointed with oil many who were sick and cured them.

Without Conflict
There Is No Story

George Anderson wanted to write a book. He had the subject of his book in mind. The title would be *Handling Troubles*. He knew that if he could get a publisher, the book would help other people. He knew he could do it, but he didn't know how, so he joined a writers' group.

A famous and successful author was addressing a group of novice writers at the writers' group meeting. The would-be writers, including George, hung on his every word. "There must always be conflict," the speaker said. "Conflict is the presenting problem, the nerve, of all good fiction. As a matter of fact, without conflict, there is no story."

George found himself thinking about that. He was a pastor. As he thought about all the people who had shared their life stories with him, he realized the truth of the speaker's point. All the people he knew had conflicts. He had them too. Currently, he was having a conflict with one of his church council members. "Conflict isn't necessarily bad," he thought. "It all depends on how you handle it." Then George thought about Jesus and the stories in scripture. "Lots of conflicts there," he thought.

In good fiction, there must always be some kind of conflict. In the world of the Bible, which is not fiction, we see the same principle at work. There is always conflict. God created us, but we rebelled and disobeyed him — conflict.

Abraham was called by God to leave his home country, his comfort zone — conflict. Moses was called to go back to Egypt, from which he had fled. He was called to confront Pharaoh. He was called to lead the Jewish people out of bondage. Conflict occurred over and over again. Isaiah had conflict. So did Jeremiah and all the prophets. So did Jesus.

In Mark 6:1-6a, we see that Jesus, in the midst of conflicts with the religious establishment, also had a major conflict in his hometown, even with his own family. At first astounded, the townspeople began to turn against Jesus as they began to say to one another, "Is not this the carpenter, the son of Mary and brother of James and Joses and Judas and Simon, are not his sisters here with us?" Mark reports, "And they took offense at him" (Mark 6:3). Conflict was beginning to brew.

When Jesus said, "Prophets are not without honor, except in their hometown, and among their own kin" (Mark 6:4), the brewing conflict boiled over. It moved from serious confrontation to explosive violence. Resentment and hatred filled the air like a blinding fog.

According to the same story in Luke's gospel (Luke 4:16-30), the additional details missing from Mark's account show resentment, hatred, and violence. "After preaching on the prophet Isaiah, Jesus said that the text was fulfilled in him, offending many of the people in the synagogue because the Isaiah text (Isaiah 61-1-2) was about the hated Gentiles being included in God's plans for a jubilee celebration related to the coming Messiah.[1] Controversy upon controversy about the Gentiles and the coming Messiah caused a major reversal from the initial cheerful good reception. The atmosphere of hospitality for a hometown boy preaching in the hometown congregation moved to the accusation, "Just who do you think you are?" Murmuring replaced greetings of welcome.

Jesus' comments got things stirred up. They got more

stirred up when Jesus, looking into the eyes of the people and reading their minds, added, "Doubtless you will quote to me this proverb, 'Doctor, cure yourself!' And you will say, 'Do here also in your hometown the things that we have heard you did in Capernaum' " (Luke 4:23).

Going from bad to worse, the crowd entered a kind of mania as they shouted slurs against Jesus and pushed and shoved him in front of them, headed for a hill. The Luke text suggests that some of the members of Jesus' family were in that crowd. Were they trying unsuccessfully to protect him or were they part of the mania against him? We don't know, but this much is clear: Jesus' family members were in that synagogue crowd. The mob reached the end of a cliff and were about to push Jesus over when he suddenly turned and looked directly at the mob leaders, with a look of absolute authority, as if it was his to command. Then Jesus just "walked through the midst of them," like a general walking through his troops. What a sight it would have been to be there, see that look, and watch that reversal!

Heightened conflict filled the air. Conflict personified was suddenly resolved by the look of the Lord God incarnate in the person of Jesus Christ. There isn't much I wouldn't sell to buy a ticket to that drama, but of course, no such thing is possible, except in a certain sense of sanctified imagination carrying us there. The story can draw us in as participants, not as audience. As the Spirit of God works in us, we can be there in our minds. We can feel the conflict and resolution. Jesus just walked right through them, like he walked on water. He commanded the violent mob like he commanded the violent wind and waves. Suddenly, there was quiet astonishment, as if God himself was present. He was.

That Jesus calmed a violent mob or a violent storm shows his power in the face of conflict. That Jesus is in charge of the universe and he promises to be powerfully present with his disciples is a great encouragement. Believers are victors, or "more than conquerors," as Saint Paul says (Romans 8:37), not because they have no conflict, but because Jesus befriends them in conflict and overcomes it.

Disciples have conflicts. After Jesus' conflicts with his family, he gave instructions to his disciples as they were directed to go out on missions for him. In Mark 6:6b-13 we hear that Jesus' disciples dealt with conflicts galore as they went out on missions for the Lord. Jesus told them of the conflict before they went out. He said, "If any place will not welcome you or listen to you, leave that place and shake the dust off your feet as a testimony against them" (Mark 6:11).

In Luke's gospel there are more details in the account of the sending of the disciples on mission. If it is the same mission commission, and not a separate one,[2] Jesus sent out seventy disciples, in partnerships of two, to go ahead of him into the towns where he would be going (Luke 10:1). "The harvest is plentiful, but the laborers are few," Jesus said. "... Go on your way. See, I am sending you out like lambs into the midst of wolves" (Luke 10:3). I'd say that's a firm prediction of conflict. The story gets more exciting because of the opposition of the enemies to be faced.

The demonic forces trying to keep the kingdom actions of these early Christians from fulfillment are great. Colossal conflict awaits the disciples of Jesus. "In this world you will have trouble," Jesus promised. He also said, "Take heart, I have overcome the world" (John 16:33 NIV). Whether people believe it or not, whether they like it or not, whether they oppose it or not, whether they raise havoc against God's disciples or not, when the disciples of Jesus go out on mission, the kingdom of God comes near to those who hear the gospel message (Luke 10:11). Conflict may come, but God's kingdom is stronger than all opposition, including the kingdoms of the world.

In the light of the story of Jesus and his disciples and the conflicts that characterize their stories, we should not expect that being Christian disciples today will be easy, peaceful, and devoid of conflicts, but we do. We are often surprised when with family, friends, or people who are outside the faith, we face conflict. We are often surprised when in society or even in the church, which is supposed to be a preview of the kingdom of God, we discover and have to deal with conflict. "It shouldn't be that way," novice Christians say. "That's the way it is," more veteran Christians respond. "We are all sinners. Where there is sin, there will be conflict."

A new Christian, let's call her Amanda, came into the pastor's office with a startling announcement. "I quit," she said. "I quit the church. I just joined a few weeks ago, but I can't stand it any longer. I quit." Fortunately the pastor had been a pastor for a long time. He thought that Amanda might have some false expectations about her newfound faith. He didn't try to argue her away from her conviction that her entrance into the world of Christians was over. He just responded, "Can you tell me about it?"

"Yes," she said, "but don't try to talk me out of it. I quit. That's it."

"I promise," he said. "Let me just listen to your story."

"In the pastor's class I took before joining this church, you said that Christians have peace that passes understanding. You promised that my life, and the life of non-believers, would change and improve by accepting Jesus as Lord and Savior. You said that I would be happy and successful. I gave it four weeks. It didn't work. I quit."

"Amanda, are you sure you heard me say those things?"

"I think that's what you said. At least, that's what I heard."

The pastor then responded, "Before we go back to what I said or what you heard, are you willing to fill me in a little more about your background and your need for help? Can you tell me some of the conflicts you have had or are having?"

After an hour of sharing with the pastor about her upbringing outside the church and her feeling inferior to others and ignorant around Christians, Amanda burst into tears. She said, "Pastor, I was raped a month before I started coming to church. I feel awful about myself. I know in my head that the rape wasn't my fault, but I still feel guilty and dirty about what happened to me. I need help. I came to the church looking for help. Instead, I've just gotten more conflicts added to the ones I had before I came to church. Not only has my family rejected me because I've become a Christian; in addition, there are some nasty women at work who are calling me names like 'holier-than-thou Mandy.' I can't stand it any longer."

"Amanda, we can get you into a rape counseling group I know about. We can also get you into a women's prayer and Bible study group where the women will be able to help you. I happen to know that some of the women in that group have suffered sexual abuse. They have helped other younger women, like you, who have suffered abuse."

"Pastor, you are so kind to offer all this. I know I should have sought help with the rape, but I was afraid others would look down on me if they knew this happened and as far as the prayer group goes, I'm so ignorant of the Bible and the ways of Christians, I'm totally uptight about attending a group like that."

"Would you be willing to come to the Bible study group if Mary attended with you? She's your friend, isn't she — the one who first brought you to church? Would you be willing to try it? If you don't like it, you can always quit."

"Well, if Mary will go with me, I guess it wouldn't hurt to give it a try."

"Good, and if you are willing, I'll give you the name and phone number of the contact person at the rape counseling group. You can contact her whenever you are ready."

"I would be willing to take the name and number. I'm not sure I have the courage to contact her, but I'll think about it."

"Would you mind if I pray with you?"

"That's fine, just don't ask me to pray out loud. I'm not ready for that."

After the pastor prayed for Amanda, she started toward the door. "One more thing. If you'll let me stay as a member, I'll try to do better. I really want to be a Christian. I just need help. I'm lonely and filled with stress. And by the way, I guess you never really said those things I said at the beginning. I just heard what I wanted to hear."

"Amanda, just remember, God loves you more than you can imagine. He wants the best for you and he won't ever desert you. It isn't easy to be a Christian today because we live in a culture that opposes much of what Christians teach, but I believe in you and God believes in you. You have great potential to be a fine disciple of the Lord. We just have to get you through this very difficult period of stress which is very real. Here is a Bible verse for you to take with you. You might want to use it every morning in your prayers and memorize it. The Bible verse is John 16:33 (NIV). "Jesus said, 'In this world you will have trouble. But take heart, I have overcome the world.' "

Three weeks later Amanda came back to see the pastor. She said, "The group you sent me to has been wonderful. They have really welcomed me. I thought I'd feel awkward, and I did a little at first, but Mary being there really helped and the other women were very supportive. One of them even took me out to dinner and listened to my troubles and conflicts. I'm feeling a lot better since I talked to you three weeks ago."

The pastor responded, "I'm really glad that the group has helped you. Sometimes, just being with other Christians who listen to your story helps to sort things through. Conflicts come to all of us. How we come out is not so much what happens to us as how we respond to what happens to us. We usually respond better to our conflicts if we have understanding people with whom we can share what is happening to us. That's what the community of the church is all about. In the Bible, that special fellowship in Christ is called *koinonia.*"

"That's a new word for me. There are lots of new things in the church I don't know about, but I want you to know more and believe it or not, I memorized that Bible passage about Jesus overcoming the world. I haven't gotten over that terrible experience I had a few months ago but I have set up an appointment with the rape counseling center and I will be going to see someone there this week. That Bible passage you gave me has really helped. I say it every morning."

"I have another one for you," the pastor said. "It's Jeremiah 29:11. 'For surely I know the plans I have for you, says the Lord, plans for your welfare and not for harm, to give you a future with hope.' " The pastor handed her the verse on a card. "Just remember, that doesn't mean you won't have troubles or conflicts. On the contrary, everyone, Christian or atheist, has conflicts that must be faced. Conflict is a part of every person's story. This passage just means that when you have troubles and conflicts, you won't have to deal with them alone. God will be right there, going through whatever you go through with you."

"Yes, I know," she said. "In this world I have troubles. But Jesus has overcome the world."

---

1. Jubilee (Isaiah 61:1-2) derived its name from the custom of proclaiming it by a blast of the trumpet. On the tenth day of the seventh month every fiftieth year the Jubilee trumpet was sounded. It proclaimed liberty for all Israelites who were in bondage. It was a time of new beginnings for the Jews and for the land.

2. The two mission commissionings in the gospels of Mark and Luke appear to be the same story. Luke gives more detail than Mark who typically is brief in describing Jesus' actions.

Proper 10
Pentecost 7
Ordinary Time 15
Mark 6:14-29

King Herod heard of it, for Jesus' name had become known. Some were saying, "John the baptizer has been raised from the dead; and for this reason these powers are at work in him." But others said, "It is Elijah." And others said, "It is a prophet, like one of the prophets of old." But when Herod heard of it, he said, "John, whom I beheaded, has been raised." For Herod himself had sent men who arrested John, bound him, and put him in prison on account of Herodias, his brother Philip's wife, because Herod had married her. For John had been telling Herod, "It is not lawful for you to have your brother's wife." And Herodias had a grudge against him, and wanted to kill him. But she could not, for Herod feared John, knowing that he was a righteous and holy man, and he protected him. When he heard him, he was greatly perplexed; and yet he liked to listen to him. But an opportunity came when Herod on his birthday gave a banquet for his courtiers and officers and for the leaders of Galilee. When Herodias' daughter came in and danced, she pleased Herod and his guests; and the king said to the girl, "Ask me for whatever you wish, and I will give it." And he solemnly swore to her, "Whatever you ask me, I will give you, even half of my kingdom." She went out and said to her mother, "What should I ask for?" She replied, "The head of John the baptizer." Immediately she rushed back to the king and requested, "I want you to give me at once the head of John the Baptist on a platter." The king was deeply grieved; yet out of regard for his oaths and for the guests, he did not want to refuse her. Immediately the king sent a soldier of the guard with orders to bring John's head. He went and be-

headed him in the prison, brought his head on a platter, and gave it to the girl. Then the girl gave it to her mother. When his disciples heard about it, they came and took his body, and laid it in a tomb.

The Pointer

John, the cousin of Jesus, baptized Jews in the Jordan River for the forgiveness of sins. He pointed to sin to prepare people for the coming Messiah. John the Baptist might also be called, John the Pointer.

In the gospel of Mark, we read that the ministry of John points to the beginning of the good news of Jesus Christ, the Son of God. John prepared the way for the coming of Jesus (Mark 1:1-2) by pointing. John pointed away from himself to the Lord Jesus Christ. It's not an exaggeration to say that John the Baptist might best be called "John the Pointer." He pointed out the sins of the people and forgiveness of those sins through Jesus Christ. John's preaching included pointing out the specific sins of King Herod.

In Mark 6:14-29 we hear about John the Baptist being sent to prison for his preaching about Herod's sins with Herodias.[1] John was arrested because he was pointing to the coming messianic king (a threat to Herod) and was pointing out Herod's sins of adultery with his brother's wife, Herodias. Herodias' daughter danced before a drunk Herod who lusted after her and promised to give her anything she wanted. Prompted by her mother, she asked for the head of John the Baptist. John's life ended when he was beheaded at the request of Salome, the lustful dancing daughter of Herodias. Pointing to the coming of Jesus and the sins of Herod and his family, John the Baptist died as the first Christian martyr. Pointing can be costly. It cost John his life.

This was not the first time that John the Baptist pointed out the sins of the people nor was it the first time John pointed to Jesus, the Savior who forgives sins. In the gospel of John, we find three dramatic descriptions of John the Baptist pointing at Jesus as the way of forgiveness and eternal life.

First, John the Pointer, when asked who he claimed to be, said, "I am the voice of one crying out in the wilderness, 'Make straight the way of the Lord' " (John 1:23). Here, John pointed to Jesus as the messianic Lord.

Predicted in Isaiah 40:3, the Baptist went before the Messiah, preparing for his coming by helping the people see their sins and renouncing them. "Put off your selfishness and look to God as the focus of your life," John was saying. "The Messiah has arrived! The Lord himself has come!"

Second, John the Pointer, when asked about baptism said, "I baptize with water. Among you stands one whom you do not know, the one who is coming after me; I am not worthy to untie the thong of his sandal." Later John explained further, "... the one who sent me to baptize with water said to me, 'He on whom you see the Spirit descend and remain is the one who baptizes with the Holy Spirit' " (John 1:27, 33). John pointed to Jesus whose Baptism[2] was superior to any human baptism.

The baptism of John was for the Jews; the Baptism of Jesus was for everyone, Jews and Gentiles. The baptism of John was for preparation for the coming Messiah. The Baptism of Jesus was established to be a vehicle or means of grace. The baptism of John was a sign of an act of repentance by men and women. The Baptism of Jesus is a sacrament, an act of God toward us. The baptism of John was for adults only. The Baptism of Jesus was the New Testament counterpart of the Old Testament circumcision, which was for children and adults.

Third, John the Pointer, when he saw Jesus walking toward him, exclaimed in a burst of excitement, "Here is the Lamb of God who takes away the sin of the world!" The next day, upon seeing Jesus coming toward him again, John exclaimed, "Look, here is the Lamb of God!" (John 1:29, 35). John pointed to Jesus as the Lamb of God.

That Jesus is the Lamb of God assures us that forgiveness of sins is possible. All who come to God through the sacrifice of the Lamb of God on the cross are forgiven. Lambs were used by Jews in Old Testament times for sacrifice. It was believed that someone, or something, had to be sacrificed to appease God who was offended by the sins of his people. Lambs, goats, and other animals were regularly sacrificed on the altar in the temple to cleanse the sins of the worshipers. When Jesus died on the cross, Christians came to understand that animal sacrifices were no longer necessary, since Jesus died on the cross as the sacrificial Lamb of God. According to the gospel of John, John the Baptist understood the work of Jesus, sacrificing himself for God's people, even before the crucifixion.

John the Pointer helps us understand that Jesus is the messianic Lord, the one who gives us grace through Baptism and the Lamb of God who takes away the sins of the world.

John the Pointer, made the connection that many people fail to make. He connected the coming of the messianic Lamb of God with the need of the people of God to confess their sins. "It is high time to straighten up your lives by repentance," he was saying. " 'Let's pretend time' is over." People often pretend that they aren't so bad, others are worse, or they really are good by nature. "It's time to rid ourselves of the illusions of our self-righteousness," the Pointer was saying: "It's time to get real. It's time to turn from your pretense and hypocrisy and turn back to God." You can imagine that the people didn't like this confrontation with reality. That was especially true of the religious leaders.

Jesus called the Pharisees and scribes "white-washed graves," which look beautiful on the outside, but inside they are full of bones and decay (Matthew 23:27). A white-washed grave with a thin coat of paint over the outside does not hide the reality of a decaying body. John the Pointer and Jesus the Messiah were both forthright when they spoke about sin from which we need to be saved. So were Peter and Paul.

Mincing no words, Peter pointed out the sinful cultural tendencies from which the people needed to be freed by the Savior and Lord, Jesus Christ. On the day of Pentecost, Peter preached boldly:

> "Repent, and be baptized every one of you in the name of Jesus Christ so that your sins may be forgiven; and you will receive the gift of the Holy Spirit. For the promise is for you and for your children, and for all who are far away, everyone whom the Lord our God calls to him." And he testified with many other arguments and exhorted them, saying, "Save yourselves from this corrupt generation."
> (Acts 2:38-41)

In pointing out sins, Peter was clear as crystal. So was a little old lady who came home from church on Sunday morning with these words burning in her mind, "Repent, and be baptized every one of you in the name of Jesus Christ so that your sins may be forgiven." The pastor had preached on Acts 2:38. She had memorized the passage.

When she got past the front door, she discovered a robber in her house. She looked him straight in the eye and said, "Acts 2:38," urging him to repent and receive new life through Jesus Christ. He froze. She called the police. As the police were taking the robber away, they asked why he stopped what he was doing when she quoted the Bible passage, Acts 2:38. "Bible passage?" he responded. "I thought she said she had an ax and two .38s."

In Acts 2:38 Peter points out two things. He points to Jesus as the way to new life and he points to repentance of our sins as the way to appropriate what Jesus has accomplished on the cross. On the cross, Jesus said, "It is accomplished." Jesus accomplished salvation for all people, but not all people receive what Jesus has accomplished for them. What is missing for many people is repentance. When it comes to salvation, we don't accomplish anything. By repentance we can appropriate what Jesus has accomplished.

Like Peter, Paul lifts high the same double emphasis of human sin and salvation through Jesus Christ alone. That double emphasis is called the law and the gospel. In Philippians 2:14-16, Paul writes:

> Do all things without murmuring and arguing, so that you may be blameless and innocent, children of God without blemish in the midst of a crooked and perverse generation in which you shine like stars in the world. It is by your holding fast to the word of life that I can boast on the day of Christ that I did not run in vain or labor in vain.

Holding fast to the word, like John, Peter, and Paul, we point to Jesus, not ourselves.

We are called to point to Jesus, but we are also called to point to the sins of our culture, our own sins, and those that surround us. On his retirement Sunday, one pastor put it this way: "I have tried to point out our sins, but before pointing to the sins of anyone else or the sins in our culture, I have been preaching these many years about my own sins and my need for forgiveness. That is our condition, yours and mine. We need forgiveness. First and foremost, for these many years together, I have tried to point to Jesus Christ, the way to forgiveness, salvation, and new life."

John the Baptist pointed out the sins of the culture in which he lived. Then he pointed to Jesus, the Lamb of God who takes away the sins of the world. That sets the standard, not only for sermons by Christian preachers, but for the witness of all of God's people today and the future. It is law and gospel!

There have been times in history when the emphasis of Christians has been distorted in favor of law. In these times, hell, fire, and damnation sermons by pastors have distorted the Christian message. Rules and regulations, when considered alone, cause the grace of God in Christ to be marginalized. Today, however, the emphasis has shifted so that what is offered in many churches is a watered-down gospel without law, such as what Dietrich Bonhoeffer, in his classic book *The Cost of Discipleship* calls cheap grace. Cheap grace is grace without commitment. An "anything goes, do as you please gospel" is no gospel at all. Without acknowledgment of our sins and repentance for those sins, there cannot be new life through Jesus Christ. That's why we point to law and gospel.

It is both sin and salvation through Christ, not one or the other, that form the paradoxical truth for new life. One emphasis without the other is a lopsided half-truth. We are called today to point to sins, starting with our own sins. Beyond sin, we are called to point to Jesus, our Lord and Savior.

Stephen, one of the deacons in the early church, sets a great example before us today. He was a pointer to both sin and salvation. As Stephen was being stoned to death by those who rejected Christ, he told the story of the patriarchs and heroes of the Bible who had followed God's will in spite of the hard-heartedness of the people (Acts 6 and 7). He pointed to Christ who followed God's will and offered salvation to all who believed. He pointed out the sins of those who rejected the Lord, including many who were condemning him to death for preaching that Jesus was Lord and Messiah.

With a sudden turn in his speech from historical description of Abraham, Moses, and the prophets, Stephen shifted to the current reality of sin: "You stiff-necked people, uncircumcised in heart and ears, you are forever opposing the Holy Spirit, just as your ancestors used to do" (Acts 7:51). When they heard these words, Stephen's persecutors were enraged. They picked up stones and started to throw them at him. While Stephen was being stoned to death, he looked up to heaven and saw an amazing sight. He saw Jesus standing at the right hand of God (Acts 7:56). We say in the Apostles' Creed that Jesus is *sitting* at the right hand of God. Why was he standing? Hold that story in your mind for a moment as we look at another story from our time. This new story may help us understand this vision of Jesus standing.

A boy genius was playing the violin in Carnegie Hall in New York City. It was such a wonderful performance that the applause was deafening as he left the stage. The stage manager said, "Great work, young man. Now, go back out on the stage. The audience wants you back."

"I can't go back out," the young violinist replied.

"Why not?" asked the stage manager. "The people want you back."

"I just can't."

"You must. They are beginning to stand and applaud. They want to give you a standing ovation."

"No. I won't do it."

"Why won't you go back out? The people are all standing and applauding. They are demanding that you return."

"There is a man in the back row in the balcony who is still sitting."

"One man? What difference does he make?"

The boy sighed and said, "He is the only one who counts. He is my teacher."

Just then, the man in the back row stood and applauded

vigorously and the violinist returned to the stage and humbly bowed.

What if Stephen, the martyr, saw Jesus not only standing, but applauding? What if Stephen understood what we often forget — that the only one who really counts is Jesus? What if, as we confess our sins and point to Jesus as the one who really counts in life, we see beyond what seems to be to ultimate reality in heavenly places, the way things really are? What if in our mind's eye we see the Lamb of God who takes away the sin of the world affirming us, applauding us? If Jesus, our teacher and our Lord, is standing and applauding you for your pointing to biblical truth, wouldn't that be the most important thing that you could ever see? Wouldn't that change you and the way you live?

A French bishop told the story of a group of young ruffians who stood outside a beautiful French cathedral where people were standing in line to make their confession of sins. The young ruffians were saying to the Christians who stood in line, "So, you think you are sinners, do you? Well there is no such thing as sin. That's just a gimmick that churches use to get you to feel guilty." One young man, who was the leader of the gang, added, "So, you believe in Jesus, do you? Well, Jesus never died on the cross for your sins. That's just something the priests and pastors made up to get you to come to church." One of the boys turned to the leader and said, "I dare you to go into the church and tell the priest what we've been saying."

"I'm not going to do that," the leader said.

"Your not afraid, are you?" said his friend.

"Of course not," the boy replied.

When the boy got to the priest, he blurted out, "My friends and I have been outside the church telling the people in line that this stuff about Jesus and forgiveness of sins is a lot of bunk. My buddy dared me to come in and tell you what we were saying. There, I've done it. Good-bye, old man."

"Wait a minute," said the old priest. "I have a dare for you as well. I want you to walk down the aisle of the church, go to the front, look up at Jesus on the cross, and say, 'Jesus died for me and I don't give a damn.' "

"I don't want to do that," the ruffian said.

"You're not afraid, are you?" asked the priest.

"Of course not," the boy shouted.

The boy ran down the aisle and shouted, looking up at the large crucifix, "Jesus died for me and I don't give a damn." He ran back to the priest and said, "I did it. Now I'm out of here."

"Not yet," said the wise priest. "Do it again."

"I don't want to do it again."

"Not afraid are you?"

"No, I'm not afraid."

Walking down the aisle, the boy finally got to the altar area, looked up into the face of Jesus, and said, "Jesus died for me and I don't give a damn."

He walked down the aisle and said to the priest, waving good-bye, "That's it. I did it."

"One more time," said the wise, old man of God pointing to the crucifix. "Then you can leave."

The ruffian slowly walked down the center aisle of the cathedral. When he got up front, he looked up, dropped his head, and said, "Jesus died for me on the cross…" He choked on each word.

The bishop who told the story, pointed to a high crucifix, and said, "I am that boy."

---

1. Herodias was the object of Herod the tetrach's guilty passion and lust while both were married to other people. Herod broke up both marriages to have the object of his lust. John the Baptist condemned the guilty pair. Herodias took revenge by plotting the death of John the Baptist.

2. The Baptism of Jesus is capitalized in this section to distinguish it from other kinds of baptism mentioned in the Bible, including John's baptism. The sacrament of Baptism, established by Jesus is different than the baptism of John called "a baptism of repentance" (see Acts 19:1-3).

Proper 11
Pentecost 8
Ordinary Time 16
Mark 6:30-34, 53-56

The apostles gathered around Jesus, and told him all that they had done and taught. He said to them, "Come away to a deserted place all by yourselves and rest a while." For many were coming and going, and they had no leisure even to eat. And they went away in the boat to a deserted place by themselves. Now many saw them going and recognized them, and they hurried there on foot from all the towns and arrived ahead of them. As he went ashore, he saw a great crowd; and he had compassion for them, because they were like sheep without a shepherd; and he began to teach them many things…. When they had crossed over, they came to land at Gennesaret and moored the boat. When they got out of the boat, people at once recognized him, and rushed about that whole region and began to bring the sick on mats to wherever they heard he was. And wherever he went, into villages or cities or farms, they laid the sick in the market-places, and begged him that they might touch even the fringe of his cloak; and all who touched it were healed.

Chaos and Solitude

Everywhere Jesus went, people flocked to him. They wanted what he was offering. They wanted inspiration. They wanted healing. They wanted God. Mark's gospel tells us that "so many people were coming and going they (Jesus and the apostles) did not even have a chance to eat" (Mark 6:31). That coming and going provided a chaotic atmosphere for Jesus' ministry. That chaos meant that even before Jesus got to a town, the mass of admirers and hangers-on rushed ahead of him and waited for his arrival (Mark 6:33). Mark points out that people "ran throughout that whole region of the Gennesaret and carried the sick on mats to wherever they heard he was" (Mark 6:55).

In dramatic contrast to all this chaos, Mark simultaneously reports that Jesus said to his apostles, "Come with me by yourselves to a quiet place and get some rest. So they went away by themselves in a boat to a solitary place" (Mark 6:31b-32).

Chaos came to Jesus because people were attracted to him. The needy and the sick came to him. The people who were looking for an authentic relationship with God came to him. The people who wanted to hear the truth about life came to him. Jesus was a man people flocked to like tiny pieces of metal attracted by a magnet. That caused a mob atmosphere much of the time. That caused chaos. Nobody could protect Jesus from the crowds. Everyone wanted a piece of him. The poor and downtrodden wanted him to help them. The sick and suffering wanted healing from him. The lonely wanted fellowship with him. That made for one chaotic incident after another as the Lord moved from place to place. People were fascinated by and attracted to Jesus.

People were attracted to Jesus' integrity. Jesus was a man who said what he would do and did what he said. There were so many hypocrites around, people who said one thing and did something else, that Jesus stood out like light in the darkness. Many of the religious leaders fell into this unhappy category. They told the people what to do, but didn't do what they told others to do. They majored in minors, emphasizing man-made rules while neglecting God's laws and God's kingdom values. Jesus confronted them and faced them down on many occasions. People marveled that Jesus stood up to the political and religious establishment.

People were attracted to Jesus' authority. "No one speaks like this man," people reported. "He speaks with authority." Jesus held no office, but he spoke like a king. Jesus had no official position, yet he spoke like one accustomed to winning. Jesus had no wealth, yet he acted like a lord and master whose vineyard was the world. Where others reacted, Jesus always seemed to take the initiative. Even nature bowed down before him. The apostles, who followed him day and night, were constantly amazed by his commanding actions over people, situations, and nature. During a storm on the Sea of Galilee "... they were filled with great awe and said to one another, 'Who then is this that even the wind and waves obey him?' " (Mark 4:31). No one was like him, before or since. There was a powerful aura around him. People sensed it and saw it. When Jesus spoke, people heard truth spoken with authority.

People were attracted to Jesus' message of love, hope, and compassion. He not only taught that we should love God above everything else and our neighbors as ourselves; Jesus lived what he taught. You could warm your hands at the love he showed to the woman with an issue of blood, Jairus' daughter (Mark 5:21-43), and the 5,000 hungry people who were fed with a few leftovers (Mark 6:1-12). Jesus fed the multitude like a caring mother feeds her beloved children. Jesus showed that same kind of love to hundreds of other people. You could see the love in his eyes as he moved among people.

You could also see hope in his eyes. He was the most hopeful man that anyone had ever seen. Hope radiated from his words and from his being. He helped people overcome physical, mental, and spiritual problems by holding out hope in front of them. "Be not afraid," he often said. He saw the future that people could have if they would just turn back to God, and he held that future up in front of their eyes so they too could see it. Healing the blind, the deaf, the mute, and even the demon possessed, Jesus lifted up hope for one and all everywhere he went.

In the eyes of Jesus you could also see something else — compassion. Where many others looked down at people, thinking themselves superior, Jesus always seemed to look out at people, from their level. Even the children, who were diminished by the culture, were treated as valuable people by Jesus. Children, as well as adults, flocked to Jesus because of the compassion they saw in him.

A little six-year-old boy was in a restaurant with his mother and father. After the adults had ordered their meal, the waiter turned to the little boy and said, "And, sir, what would you like to order?" The boy turned to his father and said, "He thinks I'm real." So does Jesus, son. So does Jesus.

With integrity and authority like he had, Jesus could have commanded governments and armies. Instead, he commanded peoples' respect and love. He still does. That's why people flock to him yet today.

With a message of love, hope, and compassion, Jesus was so unique that multitudes wanted to be where he was. They still do. If we could just get all of the human aspects of religion out of the way and help people see Jesus, their lives would be changed. "We would see Jesus," Greek seekers said (John 12:21 KJV). So would people today. Some people are attracted to Jesus because of what they hear about him or see in him. Multitudes of seekers make for chaos. So do multitudes of users.

Some people seek to use Jesus for their own ends. Just like some folks use friends or associates for their own selfish gain, like some people use the church just to get something, so some people come to Jesus trying to use him for their own ends. Often Jesus turned the tables on those who were trying to use him, for example the rich young fool and the lawyer who tried to test him with the question, "Who is my neighbor?" The Pharisees, Sadducees, and the scribes who tried to trick him were often tricked by their own words. Some people still come to Jesus trying to use him for their own purposes. It never works. It just results in more chaos.

According to Mark 6:34, the people around Jesus were like sheep without a shepherd. Matthew 9:36 reports the same thing in a slightly different way. There we read that the crowd was harassed and helpless. Many people there were frightened, anxious, confused, and defenseless. Ever feel that way? Ever experience the chaos that abounds all around us? Chaos is catching. Have you ever succumbed?

There is no doubt that there is chaos in the world we live today. The speed at which we live, the noise that surrounds our days, the pressures, the stress, the expectations — realistic and unrealistic — people have for us today, the demands that blow our minds, the hectic pace of modern life all combine to make up the mad, mad world in which we live. In our busy, chaotic, and hectic lives, we need to see the one who touched the minds, hearts, and wills of thousands of people when he came to visit our chaotic world. Chaos is catching, but Jesus did not succumb.

There was chaos all around him because so many wanted to see him, touch him, and hear him. But there was a serenity within him that people could sense. Jesus was and is the still point in a chaotic and churning world.

Jesus said, "Come away to a deserted place all by yourselves and rest a while" (Mark 6:31). Jesus knew that life includes heavy demands and hard work. Life has to have a counterpoint of rest, a time of recouping, and a healthy rhythm. Without that rhythm, life can become distorted, disheveled, and diseased. People in the marketplace must be balanced by meeting God in a quiet place. That's why Jesus took his disciples to a deserted place, a place of solitude.

Jesus' disciples had just returned from a mission of preaching and teaching the word of God. They had been involved in healing many diseases. The preaching, teaching, and healing had taken something out of them. They needed to have something put back into them. They needed some time to speak with God in order to be effective when they spoke for God. We are like them in this respect.

Actors have intermissions. Baseball players take a seventh inning stretch. Football players need a half-time break. Christians need meaningful intermissions in their lives too. We need time to refresh ourselves in the presence of God. Daily devotions can be that kind of break away from work. Prayer is the proper balance for work. Retreat can lead to a more meaningful re-entry. When that retreat is more than just a rest, when it is intentionally centered in God, it is called solitude.

To meet life's chaotic demands, we need some kind of retreat, a time of solitude with God. A retreat leader put it this way to a group of church leaders: "We are here to retreat by being with God so that we can re-enter the ministry of really being with God's people." Then he went on to do a spiritual exercise with the participants called "domains, demands, and responses." He had each person on retreat list at least three domains. He said, "A domain is any place or situation where you are expected to work or be responsible." Then he went on to explain, "Leave plenty of room after each word you write because after you have written down the domains in which you are involved, I will ask you to write down the demands you experience in those domains. After that you will need to write down your responses to those demands."

For domains, people wrote down: home, work, being a good spouse, parenting, personal finances, being a good neighbor, relating to relatives, taking care of elderly parents, and several other areas of responsibility. For demands they wrote out:

Do everything for all the children;

Fix everything that breaks;

Answer all questions;

Never fail to be alert and loving;

Never make a mistake when it comes to money;

Always be kind, considerate, and compassionate;

Always be responsible, even when I am exhausted from overwork; and

Always make the right decisions.

They wrote down many additional demands they perceived were expected of them.

Then the retreat leader, said, "Now list how you responded to those expectations and demands that you or other people have placed on you." After twenty minutes of writing, the retreat leader had some of the people share what they had written. The responses included:

"I'm exhausted because I never get done."

"I feel guilty because I never get it perfect."

"I don't like myself because I always fall short."

"I get angry too quickly because I'm frustrated."

"I don't like this exercise because it makes me feel like there is no way out."

Then the retreat leader made a statement that really shook up the participants. "In most cases, you can't do anything about the domains or demands of life. You can't control what happens to you. The only thing you really have control over is your responses." After a lot of hot discussion and argument, most of the people agreed that the real area they could change was the way they responded to what happened to them.

"You can't control what happens to you; only how you respond to what happens to you," the leader said. "And that response has a lot to do with the state of your mind and spirit." The rest of the retreat was spent on Bible reading, prayer, and discussion of attitude and perspective in the light of what God revealed in his word. One woman, who had earlier identified a problem she had with criticizing others, came up with a formula that the group liked. "I think the best way to summarize what I need to work on in my life is 'The attitude I need daily is gratitude.' "

"I've been blaming others for what goes wrong in my life," a man who said he drank too much, chimed in. "I haven't wanted to take responsibility for my own life. If the only thing I can change is my responses, that means I have to take responsibility for what happens. That isn't easy, but with God's help, I will try to change."

A husband observed, "I guess you are all right about this business of having an attitude of gratitude, but I don't think I can change the way I have been living for 44 years." His prayer partner said, "I'll pray for you, Harry. You pray for me too. I'm not sure I can change either, especially if I have to do it myself. But if we pray for one another, maybe God will get us over the hump."

In the context of solitude — time spent with God and with one another, many of the people on that retreat made the discovery that the illusions they had been living with had to do with trying to change other people instead of changing themselves with the help of God. Of course, not everyone got it. Joe Johnson said, "This is a waste of time. This solitude stuff is for the birds. I'm leaving." And he did. It's not clear at this time if Joe ever got it, but the point of that retreat on solitude was to make a deposit in each participant's account, a deposit that God could use to help people improve the rhythm of their lives.

In the closing devotions, the pastor, who was not the retreat leader, read Psalm 46:10, "Be still and know that I am God." He also quoted Henri Nouwen, the Roman Catholic spiritual writer: "In solitude we can slowly unmask the illusion of our possessiveness and discover in the center of our own self that we are not what we can conquer, but what is given to us. It is this solitude that we discover that being is more important than having, and that we are worth more than the result of our efforts."[1]

After commenting briefly on these words, the pastor quoted Nouwen again: "In solitude we become aware that our worth is not the same as our usefulness."[2] Then the pastor confessed, "This quote hits me right between the eyes (in my head): When we start being too impressed by the results of our work, we slowly come to the erroneous conviction that life is one large scoreboard where someone is listing the points to measure our worth."[3]

"We have retreated," said the retreat leader. "Now it's time to re-enter."

Joe Johnson, who had walked out of that retreat, later privately said to his pastor. "I shouldn't have walked out, but that retreat leader was getting to me. As president of the congregation and running my own business, I guess the stress was just getting to me. We are also having some trouble with one of our daughters who is dating a young man we think is a bum. That retreat leader was getting 'under my skin' with all his talk about solitude, demands, and responses. I usually can control the situations I'm in, but frankly pastor, I'm at overload."

"I know," Pastor Jones replied, "I've been praying for you every day since you left that retreat. I knew something was wrong." The two men then knelt down and prayed together.

----

1. Henri Nouwen, *Out of Solitude* (Notre Dame: Ave Marie Press, 1974), p. 22.

2. *Ibid.*

3. *Ibid.*, p. 18.

Proper 12
Pentecost 9
Ordinary Time 17
John 6:1-21

After this Jesus went to the other side of the Sea of Galilee, also called the Sea of Tiberias. A large crowd kept following him, because they saw the signs that he was doing for the sick. Jesus went up the mountain and sat down there with his disciples. Now the Passover, the festival of the Jews, was near. When he looked up and saw a large crowd coming toward him, Jesus said to Philip, "Where are we to buy bread for these people to eat?" He said this to test him, for he himself knew what he was going to do. Philip answered him, "Six months' wages would not buy enough bread for each of them to get a little." One of his disciples, Andrew, Simon Peter's brother, said to him, "There is a boy here who has five barley loaves and two fish. But what are they among so many people?" Jesus said, "Make the people sit down." Now there was a great deal of grass in the place; so they sat down, about five thousand in all. Then Jesus took the loaves, and when he had given thanks, he distributed them to those who were seated; so also the fish, as much as they wanted. When they were satisfied, he told his disciples, "Gather up the fragments left over, so that nothing may be lost." So they gathered them up, and from the fragments of the five barley loaves, left by those who had eaten, they filled twelve baskets. When the people saw the sign that he had done, they began to say, "This is indeed the prophet who is to come into the world." When Jesus realized that they were about to come and take him by force to make him king, he withdrew again to the mountain by himself. When evening came, his disciples went down to the sea, got into a boat, and started across the sea to Capernaum. It was now dark, and Jesus had not yet come to them. The sea became rough because a strong wind was blowing. When they had rowed about three or four miles, they saw Jesus walking on the sea and coming near the boat, and they were terrified. But he said to them, "It is I; do not be afraid." Then they wanted to take him into the boat, and immediately the boat reached the land toward which they were going.

Giving Up Control

There are two stories in John 6:1-21 — the feeding of the 5,000 and Jesus walking on water during a storm on the Sea of Galilee. These two stories answer two important questions.

First, when does $5 + 2 \times 1 = 12$? Mathematically, never. But in the story of the feeding of the 5,000, the multiplication formula works just like that: five loaves of barley bread, plus two small fish, times Jesus, the one man who is in control, equals twelve baskets of leftover bread. The key ingredient in that multiplication formula is Jesus, who when we give up control to him, works multiplications, wonders, and even miracles. Give Jesus what you have and he can miraculously make much more than you can imagine out of it. How does this miracle of multiplication happen? It can happen if and when we remember *Jesus is in control*.

Second, how can we be saved from those things in life which overtake us, overwhelm us, or otherwise threaten to undo us? When the storms of life threaten us, we can turn to the one who is stronger than we are and stronger than the storms themselves. We can't avoid the storms. They come to the good, the bad, and the indifferent. Just like God doesn't promise to keep us from the valley of the shadow of death, God doesn't promise to eliminate storms from our lives. On the other hand, God does promise that we can get through life's valleys and storms if we trust that *Jesus is in control*.

That's the message of both stories in John 1:1-21. In the

first story, the feeding of the 12,000 people, Phillip was faced with what appears to be an unsolvable problem. Seeing the large crowd, Jesus asks him, "Where do we buy bread for these people to eat?" Jesus, the apostles and at least 5,000 people[1] were out in the hill country just north of the Sea of Galilee with no towns nearby. They had not eaten for a long time. The question before Phillip seemingly has no answer. Then another one of the apostles, Andrew, made a statement that sounds like a totally inadequate solution. "There is a boy here who has five barley loaves and two fish." Then he said what everyone nearby must have been thinking: "But what are they among so many people?" Control — who is in control here? Not Phillip, not Andrew, not the hungry people, not the little boy with the lunch his mother packed up for him before he left home. Control — who is in control?

A wise man once said, "When everything else fails, go back to the instructions." That formula works in these stories and our lives. Our instructions for living are found in the Bible. The central theme of the Bible is that by faith we can turn control of our lives over to God. One theme of these two stories in Mark is that given inadequate resources, we sometimes wake up to the need to turn to Jesus, and let God be God. Given a desperate situation we may suddenly realize that our strength is too weak to handle the storm we face and that we need to turn to Jesus and let God be God. It's a matter of giving up control to the Lord who is the one who is in control in the first place.

When resources are inadequate for the task, it may dawn on us that we need to turn control of our lives over to God. God has control, of course. It's just that we fight that idea at every turn of the road. In this story, the apostles finally bring the small boy with his small resources to Jesus. There they can discover the wonderful principle of multiplication.

Like the boy and the apostles, we have only small

amounts of resources to meet big needs. The five barley loaves and two small fish, the little boy's lunch, are small indeed. Barley loaves were the cheapest kind of bread in Jesus' day. According to New Testament scholar, William Barclay, only poor people ate barley bread. Barley was usually fed to the animals. It was held in contempt by most people. Barclay says that the two small fish were about the size of sardines.[2] Those are small resources. Like the small resources in the story of the feeding of the 5,000, our resources are inadequate for many of the tasks we face today.

A little boy went forward for the children's sermon in his church. The pastor asked, "What is gray, has a bushy tail, and runs up and down trees?" The little boy thought for a moment. Then said, "It sounds like a squirrel, but since this is church, the right answer must be Jesus." It's not just in church that the right answer is Jesus; it's in all of life. Our resources are limited. Some tasks are just beyond what we can do. Jesus can and does multiply our small resources.

An unchurched, unbeliever discovered that principle of inadequate resources being multiplied by God. Until he was eighteen years old, the young man had not been in church ten times. After reading a book on the life of Jesus, just to be better informed, he began thinking seriously about his life. He even went to church a few times. Then on Christmas Day while he was sitting in a pew, God called him to be a Christian. God also called him to be a pastor. "Out of the question," he replied in his heart. "The answer is 'No.' I can't do that. I know nothing about the Bible, nothing about the church, nothing about God. I know nothing about religion." After a few moments, the young man revised his first answer. "I know this is you, God. I'm not making this up. I don't want to do this. I know that I can't do it. I'm fearful to speak in front of a few people, much less a congregation full of people. But I know this is you. So I'll try to do what you are calling me to do, but when I fail, you will see that I am right."

I know the truth of limited resources being used by God. I am the boy who said to God, "You are wrong. I can't do it. I'll try, but when I fail, you will see I am right." I was wrong. When God calls, he also supplies the gifts to do the work he wants us to do.

In spite of our meager resources, this story urges us to bring those resources to Jesus. When we bring our meager talents and gifts to the Lord, he can and does expand them. The gifts of God are potentially there in people. It's just a matter of encouraging their use by encouraging people to use what God has given them.

A story is told about an old German schoolmaster who, when he entered his class in the morning, used to remove his cap and bow ceremoniously to the boys. Someone asked him why he did this. His answer was, "You never know what one of these boys may some day become." He was right — because one of them was Martin Luther.[3]

When we bring people to Jesus, like Andrew brought the boy in the story to the Lord, we find that God can and often does work wonders with them, just like Jesus used the boy and his lunch for great and glorious purposes — feeding 5,000 people. Not only did Jesus feed 5,000 people with the meager gifts of the boy; there were twelve baskets full of fragments left over! That's what I call multiplication!

You plus money will not amount to much in the end. You plus success will soon fade. You plus a big reputation will be gone in no time at all. But if you turn your gifts over to God, if you give up trying to control all the aspects of your life and give up control of your life to God — that's a different story. You plus God can become an unconquerable partnership for this life and the next.

If it finally dawns on you that you can't control your

own life and that you need to submit your will to God's will, that's when the multiplication of small resources can begin to happen. This story urges us to remember $5 + 2 \times 1 = 12$.

A middle-aged woman was driving her friend's car when she came to a section called "Six Corners." "Six Corners" is a place where six different streets meet. The street lights control traffic with their green, red, and yellow colors. When the woman got to the middle of the six streets, she suddenly ran out of gas. Befuddled with the street lights flashing different colors, the horns blowing, and the people shouting, the woman turned to her friend and said, "You drive."

Of course, saying "You drive," to another person doesn't change much. You will still be out of fuel. But when you say, "You drive my life" to God and mean it, great things can happen. The presenting problem in life is that we think we can stay in control. If we recognize our limits, we may be at the right point to say to God, "You drive."

If the realization that our resources are inadequate and we are inadequate for the tasks before us doesn't help us wake up to the reality of God and God's boundless resources, maybe a crisis will drop us to our knees and drive us to the realization that we cannot control everything. Maybe the storms of life will cause us to wake up to reality.

"The sea became rough because a strong wind was blowing" (John 6:18).

When the storms of life overwhelm us, it may dawn on us that we need to turn control of our lives over to God. God has control long before we know it, of course. It's just that we fight that idea as if he is an enemy.

Control is one of the big messages in the second story in Mark 6. The storm comes up on the Sea of Galilee. Many of the apostles were fishermen. They had seen storms before. Yet, it was evening. It was dark and dangerous. They knew it. They were afraid of the rough waves and the violent

wind. They were more afraid when they saw a shadowy figure coming toward them, walking on top of the water. They
were terrified.

Jesus saw what was happening. Jesus had just fed 5,000
men. When they were so impressed that they wanted to make
him king, he sent his apostles off in a boat on the Sea of Galilee and started up the hill to be alone with God in prayer.
From that perch on the hill, Jesus saw what was happening
on the sea below him. The boat was in trouble. His friends
were in trouble.

It doesn't always seem to be true, but Jesus is aware of
what is going on in our lives too. When we are caught in
life's storms, he will come to us, even when it doesn't always feel that way. In another story about a big storm on this
same Sea of Galilee the apostles cried out to Jesus who was
resting in the boat, "Why are you asleep?" That's how we
feel at times. "Don't you see what is happening to us?" We
think, "Don't you care?"

The story of Jesus walking on water is about Jesus coming to where we are. That's the real miracle. Jesus moves
toward us when we are in trouble. Jesus cares about what is
happening.

When we feel that God is far off or sleeping and that
he must not care about us because bad things happen to us
even when we follow the Lord, we have the opportunity to
remember the hardest lesson of all. God is in control, not
me. God acts on his time schedule, not mine. God is stronger
than the storms of life and God cares about us as his children. Faith means waiting, trusting, depending on Jesus, not
self. When the sun is shining, our lives are going well, and
we are successful by human standards, it is easy to slip into
the heresy of self-dependency and lose sight of who really
is in control. In the very time that Jesus seems to be absent,
in the times when we are undone and it seems that we just

can't go on, sometimes the secret of life is discovered. *Jesus is in control.*

Jesus comes to us in the storms of life. Sometimes, Jesus comes as a shadowy figure we don't recognize right away. Sometimes it is only after an event or a tragedy or a storm that we can't handle, we see that Jesus comes to where we are. Sometimes it is only later, when we really think about what happened that we realize God was there, working his will and leading at the very time we thought all was lost. Sometimes God shows up by using other people in our lives. At the time storms come, we may not recognize God who may stand back in the shadows or the fog or the darkness. Sometimes we only see where God has been, not where God is.

That's what happened to Moses when he couldn't see God, but he saw "God's back parts." To see God's back parts means that you see where God has been. You see the finger-prints of God on your past, even though you don't see God's signature on your present. You may want to see God face-to-face. Instead, if you look closely, you may see that God was at work in your life through other people.

A man told his priest, "I quit. I'll never come back to church again."

"Can you tell my why?" the priest inquired.

"Certainly," the man replied. "I was up in Alaska on a fishing trip. I got lost and a major snowstorm isolated me from everyone. I prayed and I prayed to God to help me, but nothing happened. Nothing at all. That's why I'm through with God and through with church."

"But you are here; you are alive," said the priest. "What happened?"

"An Eskimo came along and saved me."

God sometimes comes to us in the form of other people, but we don't always recognize him. In our story, God showed up and answered the prayers of the desperate man in Alaska, but the man never made the connection. How many Eskimos are in your biography?

In our story, Jesus showed up as a shadowy figure who at first was not recognized by the apostles, but is soon seen for who he is. Sometimes it's later, rather than sooner that we make that discovery.

Sometimes God's timing is different than ours. The apostles wanted Jesus to get in the boat with them when they departed after the feeding of the 5,000 and the demand by the crowd to make Jesus king. Jesus had other plans. He had to deal with the crowd's demand to make him a secular king. Most of all he had to speak to God in prayer.

But from the hillside view, Jesus could see that his friends were in trouble on the Sea of Galilee. The text leads us to believe that Jesus did not come to them until they had nearly crossed to the other side of the sea — a three or four hour journey by boat. That's not the timing they expected.

Jesus saves us when the storms of life come. He may not save us when we want him to do so and he may not save us in the way we expect, but God answers the prayers of his people. Sometimes he answers, "Yes." Sometimes he answers, "No." Most often God answers, "Wait."

It is in waiting that we really get to know God. Waiting is the category of real faith, because when we wait, we recognize that we are not in control. God is in control. The psalmist wrote: "I wait for the Lord, my soul doth wait and in his word I hope" (Psalm 130:5). When your hope is in the *Lord*, not yourself, you have real faith. Isaiah 40:31 says, "Those who wait for the Lord shall renew their strength, they shall mount up on wings like eagles. They shall run and not be weary, they shall walk and not faint." When you wait for the Lord, renewal comes. Waiting for God means knowing God as he is, not as you make him in your image. Waiting is the

124

school that teaches us to know God. Knowing God is the most important thing of all, the number one thing.

Contrary to cultural expectations, the number one thing is not me; the number one thing is knowing God.

Contrary to cultural expectations, I don't have the remote control button for life in my hand. We live in a push button society and we easily get the wrong impression. We hold the remote control for the TV, the garage, the gate, the CD player, or the DVD player and we think, "I'm in control." Wrong. Button, button, who has the button? Not me. God has the remote control. That is God's revealed secret.

That revealed secret is what the Bible teaches. That revealed secret is what our two stories unveil. That revealed secret is what can be discovered when limited human resources are seen for what they are or when the storms of life force us to see that we are not in control. That is what we discover when we realize that Jesus is coming to where we are, despite obstacles that we think would keep him away.

I think I hear the still small voice of God saying, "Do you think a raging sea will keep me from getting to you? Think again. I made the sea. I own the sea. I command the sea."

When does $5 + 2 \times 1 = 12$? The answer is, "When Jesus is the one in the middle — when Jesus is in control — when we let go and let God — when the one in the middle is number one."

---

1. "Make the men sit down" (John 6:10). The number 5,000 in this story may actually be larger because the women and children there are apparently not counted.

2. William Barclay, *The Gospel of John*, Vol. 1 (Philadelphia: Westminster Press, 1956), p. 202.

3. *Ibid.*, p. 205.

Proper 13
Pentecost 10
Ordinary Time 18
John 6:24-35

So when the crowd saw that neither Jesus nor his disciples were there, they themselves got into the boats and went to Capernaum looking for Jesus. When they found him on the other side of the sea, they said to him, "Rabbi, when did you come here?" Jesus answered them, "Very truly, I tell you, you are looking for me, not because you saw signs, but because you ate your fill of the loaves. Do not work for the food that perishes, but for the food that endures for eternal life, which the Son of Man will give you. For it is on him that God the Father has set his seal." Then they said to him, "What must we do to perform the works of God?" Jesus answered them, "This is the work of God, that you believe in him whom he has sent." So they said to him, "What sign are you going to give us then, so that we may see it and believe you? What work are you performing? Our ancestors ate the manna in the wilderness; as it is written, 'He gave them bread from heaven to eat.'" Then Jesus said to them, "Very truly, I tell you, it was not Moses who gave you the bread from heaven, but it is my Father who gives you the true bread from heaven. For the bread of God is that which comes down from heaven and gives life to the world." They said to him, "Sir, give us this bread always." Jesus said to them, "I am the bread of life. Whoever comes to me will never be hungry, and whoever believes in me will never be thirsty."

When I AM Speaks, You'd Better Listen

It appears that somebody got into the front window of life and changed the price tags. The expensive things now have cheap labels. The cheap things have expensive labels. What has happened is that today we have what might be called a transvaluation of values. Everything is turned upside down. Important values have become unimportant for many people. Unimportant values have been turned into seemingly valuable categories.

Just look at the ads on television, the movies, or the magazines being produced today. From the perspective of popular media you would think that getting more and more material things is the most important thing of all and that God and the Bible are somewhere on the sideline, if we are to consider them at all. Values have been turned upside down. It has happened gradually, so many of us have hardly noticed that it has happened.

It is like the old story of the frog in the kettle. Put a frog in hot water and he will jump right out, but put him in cool water and gradually turn up the flame underneath the pan and the frog will slowly die without noticing what is happening. Our cultural path to death is like that.

The biblical corrective for this situation of upside-down values is found in the name of God — the great I AM. This is the name that God gave to Moses when Moses agreed to go to Egypt and lead the people out of bondage. "Give me your name that I might tell the people who sent me," Moses requested.

"Tell them that I AM who I AM sent you," God replied (see Exodus 3:13-15). God is the center of life. When we put something else in the center of our lives, we don't work right. God is the great I AM. We better pay attention to him — how he reveals himself and what he says.

According to the gospel of John, Jesus used the name I AM for himself on numerous occasions. In the text before us, he says of himself, "I am the bread of life" (John 6:35; also see 6:48 and 6:51). In John 8:12, Jesus says, "I am the light of the world." In John 10:7 Jesus says of himself, "I am the door of the sheep" and in John 10:11 he claims, "I am the good shepherd."

Other "I am" sayings by Jesus in the gospel of John include:

"I am the resurrection and the life" (John 11:25).

"I am the way, the truth, and the life" (John 14:6).

"I am the real vine" (John 15:1).

"Before Abraham was, I am" (John 8:58).

Space doesn't allow us to examine each of these "I am" sayings in depth, but it is obvious that in the gospel of John, Jesus identifies himself as the great I AM that Moses met in the wilderness. Jesus was a great teacher, but those who claim that he was *just* a great teacher, and not divine, have to eliminate these I am sayings from consideration. I AM is God's name. Jesus claims that name for himself. Either he is egocentric and insane, or he is what he claims to be: both God and man.

Exodus 3:13-15 puts these words into the mouth of God: "This (I AM) is my name forever, and this is my title for all generations." That is the high, holy, and exalted name God uses for himself. Jesus used that name for himself. Should he be locked up or held up high and worshiped?

In our gospel lesson for today, we hear the claim of divinity and the connection between the wilderness story of Moses and the preaching of Jesus on the theme of bread. Moses received the manna from heaven. Jesus claimed to be the manna from heaven. Moses told the people that they needed to eat the heavenly manna God sent to sustain them. Jesus said he is the heavenly manna that sustains us. Moses pointed away from himself. Jesus pointed to himself. Jesus was either an egomaniac or what he claimed to be: God incarnate. You can't limit him to being *just* a great religious leader. He was that but so much more. He was, he is, the great I AM who is the bread of life.

Since Jesus is the great I AM, that means he is in control. I am not in control, but my sinful tendency is to try to be in control. As a servant says in the parable of the master who went away to be crowned king, "We don't want this man to rule over us" (Luke 19:14). We don't want anyone to rule over us, not even God who created us. That's the biggest conflict that characterizes our days.

The entire Bible can be outlined around this theme of God's rule over us. In Genesis 1, God creates us in his own image. He commands that the fruit of one tree is out of bounds. Chapter 2 of Genesis tells us that we rebel against God's authority and eat that one forbidden fruit. Then we play the game "PTB" — passing the buck. Adam replies to God who asks him what happened, "It's her fault. She made me do it." Eve responds, "The snake is responsible." If the snake could speak, I suppose it would say, "Don't blame me. You made me that way." In other words, not only do we rebel against God's authority, but we make excuses instead of repenting for our wrong doing. Sound familiar?

The rebellion and rationalization mean that we don't

want God to rule over us. The rest of the Bible from Genesis 2 through the last verse in Revelation is about God working to restore us to God's reign over us. God works to restore us in God's way, not by forcing us under his control with power, but by inviting us back to his control for our own good.

That invitation comes to us because God gave us the option of saying "Yes" or "No" to him. We have the freedom to reject God's offer of accepting us in Christ, in spite of our rebellion, if we repent and come to him sincerely. Before we come to him, he has come to us by the power of the Holy Spirit to create the faith we need to be saved. As Luther said, "I cannot of my own reason or strength believe in Jesus Christ or come to him, but the Holy Spirit called me by the gospel, enlightened me with his gifts, sanctified and kept me in the true faith...."[1] While we are fighting the rule of God over us for our own good, God is at work in us to bring us back into the fold. That's the classic battle in our souls between God and the devil.

God has accomplished our salvation by Jesus dying on the cross. Inspired and prodded by the Holy Spirit, we are called to appropriate what God in Christ has accomplished. From the cross Jesus said, "It is accomplished." It's like a gift of a million dollar check being given to us by God's grace. It has been given, but unless we turn it over and sign it, we don't receive the benefits of that gift. Some foolish and stubborn people refuse to sign the check. They refuse to listen to the great I AM. Instead, they put other things in first place and thereby commit idolatry.

As mentioned earlier, many people have turned the biblical values on their head. They value things that are cheap and devalue things like faith that are precious. That's happening in our culture. In addition, in many churches, we have so emphasized the horizontal dimension of Christianity that we have neglected the vertical dimension. The horizontal dimension is the human relationships we have, the need to respect one another, serve one another, and love one another. In many churches, the social gospel has replaced the gospel of salvation through Christ alone. In other words, the emphasis on the horizontal dimension of our faith is true enough, but not big enough. The whole truth is contained in the biblical admonition, "You shall love the Lord your God with all your heart and with all your soul and with all your strength and with all your mind and your neighbor as yourself" (Luke 10:27).

The whole truth, the big enough truth, is that we are called to love the Lord our God above and beyond anything else. That is the vertical dimension so often neglected today. Our text provides a corrective by reminding us that Jesus is the great I AM and the bread of life. The great I AM is in charge. That we are called to love our neighbors is a corollary to loving God first.

From the perspective of the gospel of John, there are two options in life: either I am in charge, or I AM is in charge. When I am is in charge, life doesn't work the way it was designed. When I AM is in charge, life works the way it is supposed to work according to God's plans and purpose.

When I am in charge, I consistently mess things up, make excuses for the mess I make, and refuse to take responsibility for what goes wrong. In other words, the biggest problem I have in life is that I am self-centered. The center of the word "sin" is I. That's the problem we all have. We can't get ourselves out of the center, even when we try hard. No act of the self can lift the self out of the self because the self is the problem. Unless that which is above us rules that which is within us, that which is around us will. In other words, we get trapped in one idolatry after another when we don't submit to the lordship of Jesus Christ, the great I AM.

Harold was trapped in alcoholism. They called him "Hap," short for happy, because he was a happy drinker. As far as most people knew, "Hap" was a respected judge and a good family man. But "Hap" had a secret. He drank to solve his problems. When drinking became his chief problem, he drank to solve that problem too. That's the cycle of alcoholism. "Hap" claimed that he wasn't an alcoholic, and he could stop drinking any time he chose. When his life began to cave in, he tried to stop drinking, but he failed time and time again.

One day, the bills from a recent trip arrived. The trouble was that "Hap" didn't remember making that trip. He had invited his drinking buddies to fly to Chicago with him, take in a Chicago Bears football game, and eat at expensive restaurants — all at his expense. He stared at the bills and said, "I don't remember inviting my friends to go with me. I don't remember the flight to Chicago or the football game. I don't remember any of the meals we ate. But these bills prove that I did all that. Since I don't remember any of it, I know I'm out of control in my life. I give up. I acknowledge that I can't handle my life. I can't control my drinking. I give up control to you, Lord."

From that point on, as "Hap" arose every morning, he prayed, "Dear Lord, I can't handle my drinking. I commit my life and my problems to you. Without you being in control, I will only mess things up as I've done before. You are the only one who can keep me from drinking today. I turn my life over to you today, one day at a time. In Jesus' name. Amen." From that point on, for the rest of his life, "Hap" never drank a drop of liquor. As he looked back on his former life, he said, "One drink was always too much and a thousand were not enough." If you complimented him about his decision to stop drinking, "Hap" would always say, "Not me, God."

In terms of our text, "Hap" made the transition from "I am in charge of my life" to "I AM is in charge of my life." To put it another way, Jesus became the nourishment "Hap" needed for life, the food and drink that kept him alive. For the last years of his life, he listened to and depended on the great I AM. He also witnessed to the power of Jesus Christ to other people.

When the great I AM speaks, we had better listen. The great I AM has spoken. What he says is called the word of God. That word of God is primarily Jesus himself. In addition, that word is the Bible and the preaching and sharing of the gospel. Will we listen to the siren calls of the world or will we listen to the word of God and pass it on?

The answer to that question is given in a story about a bully and a wise man. The bully decided to challenge the wise man. "I have a little chick in my hands, behind my back. If you are so wise, tell me, is it alive or dead?"

Of course, the wise man knew that if he said, "Alive," the bully would kill the little chick. If he said "Dead," the bully would pull out the chicken from behind him and say, "Wrong."

The wise man said, "That's up to you."

In like manner, the answer to whether you will follow the ways of the world or the ways of the great I AM is the answer given by the wise man. "That's up to you."

---

1. Martin Luther, *The Small Catechism, The Book of Concord* (St. Louis: Concordia Publishing House, 1951), p. 161.